# MELANATED MIDLIFE

## A MANUAL FOR LETTING GO AND LEVELING UP AFTER 50

### AKILAH WILLERY

# DEDICATION

For my guys, Brian, Brian II, and Nicholas - I love you and never want you to walk a single day on this earth without knowing that for sure. These song lyrics beautifully express every prayer I have for you:

*I hope you never lose your sense of wonder*
*You get your fill to eat, but always keep that hunger*
*May you never take one single breath for granted*
*God forbid love ever leave you empty-handed*
*I hope you still feel small when you stand beside the ocean*
*Whenever one door closes, I hope one more opens*
*Promise me that you'll give faith a fighting chance*
*And when you get the choice to sit it out or dance*
*I hope you dance*
*I hope you never fear those mountains in the distance*
*Never settle for the path of least resistance*
*Livin' might mean takin' chances, but they're worth takin'*
*Lovin' might be a mistake, but it's worth makin'*
*Don't let some hellbent heart leave you bitter*
*When you come close to sellin' out, reconsider*
*Give the heavens above more than just a passing glance*
*And when you get the choice to sit it out or dance*
*I hope you dance*
*I hope you still feel small when you stand beside the ocean*
*Whenever one door closes, I hope one more opens*
*Promise me that you'll give faith a fighting chance*

*And when you get the choice to sit it out or dance*
*I hope you dance*

"I Hope You Dance"
Song performed by Lee Ann Womack
Written by Tia Sellers and Mark D. Sanders

# ACKNOWLEDGEMENTS

This book is my someday. Someday, I'll put all these ideas into action and do great things with them. Someday, I'll get the nerve to start a business. Someday, I'll publish my first book and be able to add "published author" to my CV. Someday, I'll discover that fully showing the world who I am, really, was the only option all along.

I want to thank the global Melanated Midlife community for jumping on the bandwagon of a platform built by a complete midlife rookie and growing it into something special. If you have ever listened to the podcast, read my newsletters, or shared my YouTube videos with a loved one, thank you for your support. You validated every embarrassing newbie mistake I made and gave me the encouragement to keep showing up.

I also want to thank my production team behind the podcast. When my brother-in-law, Derrick Owens, first listened to my idea and leaped into action to help out, I knew I was leaving my comfort zone behind for good. After a gazillion hours of video footage, I think we are finally starting to get the hang of it.

Several of my past podcast guests are mentioned throughout the book. Thank you to every single midlife baddie who said yes to appearing on the podcast without any hesitation, and especially for courageously sharing your stories, so each person in this community can learn how to design their dream midlife.

A huge thanks to my personal village, where I never had a single loved one talk dismissively about any crazy idea I had about starting over in midlife. If you ever nodded in agreement and gave me a gentle push forward, then I dedicate this work to you.

# TABLE OF CONTENTS

# INTRODUCTION

Welcome to your midlife design! You made it. I don't know how you got here, but I'm really grateful you stopped by. Maybe you grabbed this book on a whim, or because something deep inside whispered, "It's time." Whatever brought you here, celebrate that spark of curiosity and hope. We're in this together: a very deep, melanated diaspora of women turning fifty, professionals, mothers, and friends, each carrying stories waiting to be told.

Whether this book found you on a quiet night when you were questioning what comes next, or during a scroll between meetings and responsibilities, I want you to know this: you are exactly where you're supposed to be. You didn't pick this book up by accident. Something inside of you. Maybe it was a whisper, or a scream that said it's time. Time to rethink, to reclaim, and to realign your life with the version of you that's been patiently waiting to be seen.

This book is not a rigid blueprint that demands perfection or a ten-step plan to a brand-new you. It's a mirror and a map. It's a soft place to land and a gentle nudge forward. It's the stories, lessons, and lived truths of a woman who has been there…burned out, boxed in, full of potential but unsure what to do with it next. It's also a celebration of what's possible when we stop performing and start becoming.

I wrote this for us. For the midlifers of color who have checked all the boxes, done all the right things, and are still craving something more. More joy. More freedom. More truth. More rest. More audacity.

Inside these pages, you'll find real stories, research, hard truths, and softer reminders. You'll see your own fears reflected back, but more importantly, you'll find tools to walk through them. You'll meet women who started over in their 40s, 50s, and beyond. You'll explore your relationship with home, career, money, boundaries, and community. Plus, you'll do so in your own time, in your own way.

I'm not here to tell you what to do. I'm here to walk beside you while you figure it out. I'm here to offer perspective. I'll share the missteps and magic I've collected along my own path. I'll remind you that you are not too old and it is not too late.

Thank you for trusting me with your attention, your heart, and your hopes for this next incredible season. I don't take that lightly. So let's begin, bravely, imperfectly, and together.

For years,, I've heard a lot of chatter about the so-called dreaded midlife crisis, but around here, we call it a midlife pivot. On the *Melanated Midlife Podcast*, I say it plain: "We're going to be sharing all those stories so that you feel empowered to do the exact same thing." That podcast debuted in 2024 on YouTube and was inspired by the leap my hubby and I decided to make once we reached our empty-nest season. Our friends and family had questions and seemed genuinely interested in how this journey would play out. I was eager to chronicle and share everything we learned after taking one very scary big step. As a former educator and self-described organizational freak, I took detailed notes along the way. This very book was born out of the desire to share our process. It's just like when someone is brave enough to walk out from the sandy beach shore, and then call back to you to say, "Come on in, the water's great".

Everything about our perspective shifted when we found ourselves with more time and ideas of what we could do now that we had time. The school responsibilities were done. The mom taxi was no longer needed. Our family calendar was suddenly wide open. There was time to breathe and dream. My husband and I didn't just tiptoe into this season. We flipped everything on its ear, choosing reinvention over resignation.

Pop culture is finally catching up with folks our age. We're naming menopause, unpacking ageism, and spinning TLC and Wu-Tang on Gen Z playlists. But where is the voice that speaks directly to us? The hip-hop generation that defined "fly" is now asking, "What's becoming fly at fifty?" That question drove me to create this space, so Black professionals like us can say, "Here's what I need: encouragement, community, and a clear path for my next chapter."

We're living in what I call our sandwich era. On one side, we've poured our hearts into nurturing children toward independence. On the other side, we're bracing to support our own parents as they age. We find ourselves sitting firmly in that grey area in between. Are you feeling that squeeze?

This is a precious window of time to reclaim our identity and ask: "Who am I, now that I'm not just someone's mom or someone's employee?" I've had my season as a career person, then my season as somebody's wife, somebody's mother, somebody's employee. Now all of that is starting to shift. I'm re-evaluating who I am for myself. Right now it's feeling pretty good.

This book is meant to be a manual that you can read through and refer back to as often as needed to get your personal midlife season off the ground. It is divided into 3 sections: career, home, and self. These are the big midlife areas I want you to intentionally redesign as if you have a blank canvas in front of you. You will take a hard look at your career and whether you are short-changing yourself professionally in any way. Then you will reevaluate your home and decide where you can simplify it to make room for new priorities. Lastly, you will look in the mirror at yourself and set some boundaries to fiercely protect your peace. Assume everything is on the table and you have full control to create your midlife experience however you want. Put yourself at the top of the list of people who need to be consulted on how this season will look and feel.

So let's lean in. In this chapter, we'll move from recognizing that restless stir inside you to defining your personal pivot. We'll explore the power of nostalgia, like those first tracks of your youth that still make your heart beat faster, and how they can soundtrack your boldest moves yet. We'll give you practical reflection prompts so you can turn conversation into action.

Just like any manual or learning resource, make this book your personal cheat sheet to design what your bold, selfish midlife experience will look like. Highlight the parts that grab your attention. Scribble notes all around the pages. Post your a-ha light bulb moments on social media or share them in the friend group chat. The learning is meant to be shared with as many midlife baddies as possible.

Every chapter will teach one basic lesson for how to do this lifestyle redesign. Each chapter also contains a guided reflection activity for you to visualize your next phase. There will be action items so you can hold yourself accountable. With each reflection activity, I want you to take them to heart and really map out what your ideal midlife season might look like. I am a digital girl, but I still keep my deepest, most personal goals and thoughts in a beautiful spiral-bound journal. This allows me to take my time writing out my goals in cursive longhand with colored pens and stickers, much like an '80s middle schooler writing out song lyrics in a notebook. I invite you to do the same as you read this book. My intention is for you to fully engulf yourself in designing this season of life for yourself. Let your journal be raw and honest as you draft each layer of your dream midlife.

By the end of this book, you won't just retire from the idea of a midlife crisis. You'll own a midlife pivot of your own design, rooted in your culture, your stories, and the fierce joy you deserve next. Welcome to the Melanated Midlife remix.

As we stood on the threshold of midlife, my husband and I embraced a mantra: let's treat midlife like less of a crisis and more like an upgrade. Hitting this phase brought a whirlwind of changes, which for me was right around age 47. That's when menopause also came knocking. At first, I didn't connect the dots between all these new symptoms and that big change. As I settled into it, I realized how much of an opportunity this season could be.

With our kids heading off to college in rapid succession, the house that once buzzed with school activities and endless schedules suddenly felt a little quieter. But instead of mourning that shift, we saw it as our chance to retire from being the kid taxi and embrace a new kind of freedom. What would we do with all this time? How would we fill our days, evenings, and weekends now that they were truly ours again?

This excitement came with an awareness that this season of complete freedom might have an end date. We knew we were in that sandwich era. Just as our children were stepping into their independence, our parents might soon need more of our support. That knowledge made this time feel even more precious, which was a reminder not to put off those dreams for another day or another year.

Turning 50 didn't feel old at all. As the hip-hop generation, we still felt cool, relevant, and deeply connected to the pulse of culture. Our music, our fashion, and our global awareness were still shaping the world around us. This wasn't a crisis; it was our prime. We were at our most educated, our most financially stable, and our bravest. This was our moment to shine.

So now that you've walked alongside us into this upgrade mindset, it's your turn. Take a moment to shine the spotlight on your own season of life. What changes have quietly been stirring in you? Maybe they were symptoms you shrugged off. What routines have you outgrown, or what dreams have you paused? When you imagine this next chapter, what feels urgent, thrilling, or even a little scary?

**Your Turn: Reflect and Respond**

1. **Connect the Dots:** Think back over the past two years. What new "symptoms" or shifting feelings have you experienced? What energy dips, restless thoughts, unexpected cravings for something different have you felt? How might these be signposts pointing you toward your own upgrade?

2. **Sandwich Era Check:** List the three most time-consuming roles you play today. Which one feels most "finished," and which one feels like it's just beginning? If you could reclaim just one afternoon from those roles, how would you spend it?

3. **Upgrade Vision:** Write down one bold thing you'd do if you knew you had a finite window of freedom. No more 'someday". There is just "now." How does that choice light you up?

4. **Cultural Cue:** What piece of your personal history still sparks joy or confidence, like an old song, a favorite film, a memory from your youth? How can you lean into that energy as you sketch out your midlife upgrade?

Jot down your thoughts in the margins, in a separate journal, or on your phone. There's no right or wrong answer here. There's only the first brushstrokes of your next great chapter. Let's keep going.

Embracing the Melanated Midlife mindset means recognizing that midlife is a time of profound transformation and empowerment. At this stage in life, we've accumulated a wealth of experience and wisdom that uniquely positions us in the professional world. We understand ourselves better than ever, and we have the clarity to know what we truly want. This is also the time when our earning potential is at its peak, and we bring a depth of leadership and expertise that truly sets us apart.

However, as we navigate these transitions, it's important to remember that while our credentials and hard work are essential, they are just the foundation. The true key to unlocking new opportunities lies in building and nurturing connections. We have to move beyond the myth of a pure meritocracy and recognize that it's our networks and relationships that often open the most doors.

In addition, we need to be unapologetically clear about our financial goals. Money is a crucial part of designing the life we want, and it's important to have honest conversations about what we need financially. By understanding and articulating our financial needs, we empower ourselves to pursue opportunities that truly align with our desired lifestyle. Money might not buy happiness, but it does afford us the freedom and flexibility to live the life we envision. By embracing all of these elements, we can step confidently into this new chapter of our lives, fully empowered and ready to thrive.

Embracing the Melanated Midlife means being honest and intentional about what you truly want in this next chapter of your life. Take a moment to reflect: What are the goals that you're aiming for? What does your ideal life look like? Think about what truly excites you and what you might be ready to let go of. Remember, you're not here because you're unsatisfied or ungrateful for where you are now, but because you're ready for what comes next. Allow yourself to dream boldly and be clear about your aspirations. This is your time to design a life that truly reflects who you are and what you desire.

I am right beside you and rooting for you.

With love and understanding,

Dr. Akilah Willery

# PART ONE

## CAREER

# CHAPTER 1

## I'm Not Too Old. I'm Just Getting Started: Reclaiming midlife as a season of becoming, not fading.

L et me tell you something I wish someone had told me when I was standing at the edge of burnout, reinvention, and a whole lot of "What now?": You are not too old to start again.

I had to learn that the hard way, through exhaustion, a little disappointment, and some serious questioning of my worth and purpose. Somewhere in the mess of it all, I had an awakening: this isn't the end of anything. It's the beginning of everything I hadn't yet claimed for myself.

I wrote this book because I know what it feels like to have a career that once gave you joy, but starts to feel like a cage. I know what it feels like to wonder if you've missed your window. I've also felt the pain of secretly dreaming of doing something different, but feeling paralyzed by the thought of starting over at 40, 50, or beyond. You're not alone in that. In fact, a 2023 study from the American Institute for Economic Research found that over 1 million people over the age of 40 change careers every year, and 90% of them report feeling happier, more successful, and less stressed afterward. Reinvention is not just possible. It's powerful.

Well, friend, you're right on time. Imagine that you just sat down next to me on a long flight, and we have uninterrupted time to dive into your story, your unfulfilled dreams, and whatever it is that kept you from chasing them… until now. Yes, we have time, but that time is eventually going to run out. No, I am not going dark and morbid on you just yet. I'm not referring to the end of all your days. I'm trying to remind you that everything has a season, and this midlife journey is one of the seasons in your life. Like any season, it eases its way in, fully blooms, and then fades when it's time for a new season to take its place.

Although it is a season, it took a long while to get here. By the time we hit 50, we've been fully grown working adults for nearly three decades. You have probably carved out your place in a long career. Maybe you've been in the same organization, or at least the same profession, that entire time. How am I coming to that assumption? It's just a guess, but as Gen X, we were taught by our Baby Boomer elders that hard work and loyalty to our employer meant they would be loyal to us. We assumed that longevity and the seniority we earned would be enough to protect us in the event of an economic downturn. Job hopping was considered foolish and made you look irresponsible or flaky.

But after all that time, you find yourself wondering what else there is for you in your career. You do some quick math and realize you are way too young to head to the house for a full retirement. In fact, by the time you hit your 50s, you might have another 15–20 years of working full-time still ahead of you. And here's the thing: you're not alone in wondering if it's time for something new. A 2024 Forbes article reported that 50% of workers aged 45 and above hope to change jobs within the next three years. That statistic alone tells me you're in good company.

Midlife is not your expiration date, and it's certainly not a reason for a crisis. It's your evolution season. If you've ever whispered to yourself, "I think I want more," then this book is for you. Not because you're broken, but because you're becoming (thank you, Forever First Lady Michelle Obama). You feel restlessness with your current situation. You're questioning your commitment to what you thought you always wanted.

When I first sat down to write this book, the motivation was layered. First, like any good educator, I saw some gaps in our collective understanding of what our lives should be like once we hit 50 years old. Even now, when I say my age out loud, it feels a little weird. Outside of the audible cracks in my joints when I get out of bed each morning, I truly feel like I'm still in my late 30s. Now, let me clarify that a little better. I am not saying that I am still as physically strong as a 30-something-year-old woman. No, not hardly. My menopause beast is giving me the side eye right now. What I mean is that mentally, my awareness is still frozen somewhere in that decade.

Along this journey, I got to know Angela Trahan, K–12 district leader and empty nester. She was beginning to embrace this new chapter of life with excitement, joy, and freedom through ongoing self-discovery. The beauty of Angela's story is that she actually had all the creative ideas and answers to her deepest questions about making a big midlife pivot. However, they were buried under layers of "shoulds". She *should* be content with her career, in which she had already accomplished so much. She *should* stay conservative with her trajectory, even though becoming a certified coach was a very achievable dream move. When she and I started working together, she was able to grant herself permission to set aside all those "shoulds" and align her ambitions with finally launching her own business, which she achieved well into her 50s. She wasn't starting from step one. She was starting from years of experience and the wisdom of someone who didn't want to sleepwalk through this next phase of her life.

*"In midlife, I stopped trying to fit into other people's expectations and started embracing who I truly am. I began betting on myself (no more excuses), no more playing small. I prioritized self-care, strengthened my emotional intelligence, and committed to leading*

*with courage, clarity, and transparency. Now, when something calls to me, I don't overthink it -I just do it."*

## What happens when the OG hip-hop generation turns 50?

You know how it is when you look at celebrities in your age group and find out they have somehow reached their 50s, but you haven't? We are the OG hip-hop generation. Public Enemy, MC Lyte, The Geto Boys, Queen Latifah, N.W.A., Wu-Tang Clan, and many others were the standard back in the day. Hip hop and New Jack artists, from the East Coast to the West Coast, to the Third Coast, were the inventors of cool in my eyes. Their music, storytelling, and fashion still influence the culture today. Those tunes still dominate my workout playlist. I personally spent the early 90s as a broke-down version of a Janet Jackson disciple, and you couldn't tell me nothing, honey! I attended my first New Edition concert in the '80s and jammed to Jodeci in the '90s. Heck, my playlist today still has Mary J., En Vogue, and the Fugees on steady rotation.

The music and videos of that era are frozen in time, so I can revisit those joyful feelings at any time, thanks to streaming music services. My consciousness was born during that era. My young adulthood was influenced so deeply by the lyrics and cultural representation. We were boldly on full display back then and unapologetic about it. But when you hear about those same cultural icons today, saying their current age out loud, you think "damn, they are getting old". Then you pause and realize that you, too, are in that same age group, and your whole world tilts slightly as you let this awareness sink in.

It bleeds into my real world, too. Both my sons are in their early 20s now. Intellectually, I know this. However, when thoughts of them first hit my brain, I still see two little boys. When either one of them walks into a room (both are tall guys), it takes a moment for my mind to reconcile that these young men and my little boys are one and the same. They are in college at the moment, so they haven't started fully adulting yet. But the idea of them living their daily lives in other cities where I cannot monitor their well-being and safety can be a real head trip. How can this be? Has that much time really passed for me to have grown children? Wasn't I just in the car rider pick-up line, like yesterday?

So yeah, my dear, time has marched on. But the beauty of this is that we are much more capable of keeping up and making it work in our favor. We have many years of experience and wisdom to equip us to navigate this period in ways that bring us joy and fulfillment. Research backs this up. A 2024 survey showed that 78.5% of midlife professionals are actively learning new skills, and nearly 80% prioritize fulfillment over happiness in their careers. If you hear your own clock ticking, it is not something to fear, but instead a reminder not to waste what you have. This life is for living, and if you've found yourself here, reading this book, then you're also ready to live it to the fullest.

## The Hard-Won Lessons That Brought Me Here

All of these combined experiences taught me some painful and powerful truths. Those truths are the foundation of this book:

### You are not too old to pivot.

I had moments when I thought my age disqualified me. Maybe the best I could do was stick it out in the job I had, because it was too late to learn something new. Who would hire me at this age, and what kind of salary could I get? But midlife taught me otherwise. I wasn't too old. I was finally experienced enough to know what I wanted and bold enough to go after it. Chapter 3 will walk you through recognizing when the job no longer fits the woman, and what to do about it.

### You better keep those receipts.

For too long, I let my accomplishments fade into the background, assuming someone would notice. Spoiler alert: they didn't. That's when I started documenting everything. I'm talking about my wins, results, praise, projects, and even screenshots of "you saved the day" emails. You'll learn in Chapter 4 why collecting your receipts is not optional and how to start building your case for promotions, opportunities, and self-worth. You'll learn that not only is no one noticing what you are doing, but that these same receipts will have a deeper impact on you and how you see yourself going forward.

**They forgot what you did. Don't you dare.**

Let's be clear: no one is going to advocate for you like *you*. That's why self-promotion isn't bragging. It's a survival, and it is required in today's job market. In Chapter 5, we'll discuss how to leverage your receipts to establish your personal brand, how to present yourself online and in interviews with clarity, and how to pitch yourself with confidence instead of crossing your fingers and hoping to be noticed. If you don't learn how to tell your story well, then you are accepting the status quo because of your fear of changing it.

**Simplify to clarify.**

As I stripped away the clutter in my home, calendar, and mindset, I began to see my life and potential more clearly. That clarity gave me space to decide what I actually wanted next, and the energy to pursue it. That thread runs throughout this book, giving you permission to let go of what no longer fits so you can embrace what's trying to emerge.

**This time, it's about you.**

You've given enough. You raised the kids, showed up for the job, and played by the rules. Chapter 2 is all about dismantling the guilt of choosing yourself in midlife, and building a life that centers your joy, your peace, and your desires unapologetically. Plus, you will give yourself permission to leave behind the guilt you might be feeling for putting yourself first. This is a season to be selfish and unlearn all the habits that taught you to put everyone's needs before your own.

**It's not too late to start over. Again.**

Reinvention isn't a one-time event. It's a way of life. Chapter 6 will walk you through how to recover from burnout, disappointment, or a career loss. Instead, you will use it as fuel for a more aligned, purpose-filled path forward.

Midlife isn't a crisis. It's a crossroads. We'll discuss why you get to decide which direction you're heading next. You have likely faced many other crossroads in the past, but you probably had a lot of other people to consider then, too. Now, the time is for you and you alone. Act like it. We won't stop with just your career reinvention. Be prepared to take some hard looks at how you organize your home in this season. Are too many relics from your past keeping you stuck in ways you haven't yet realized? We'll walk through ways to simplify your home, or possibly downsize it altogether, so you can be free to follow a path where the extra baggage comes with too many costly fees.

There will also be ample opportunities to look inward and explore where you might be hemorrhaging energy because you failed to honor some personal boundaries. Maybe you've been saying yes when your body is screaming no. Maybe you've been shrinking yourself to keep the peace, overextending to prove your worth, or avoiding hard conversations out of guilt or fear. In midlife, these silent leaks can cost us more than time. They chip away at our joy, our clarity, and our power. This is your moment to take inventory. Where are your boundaries too loose, too rigid, or too undefined? The goal here isn't perfection. The goal is awareness. You deserve a life where your peace isn't constantly being negotiated. Let this be the beginning of reclaiming your time, your energy, and your emotional bandwidth with intention.

This book won't give you all the answers. But it *will* help you ask better questions. The kind that brings you back to yourself. The kind that reminds you: you're not too old, too late, or too anything. You're just getting started.

## What If the Real You Is on the Other Side of This Pivot?

Your title doesn't define you. Your worth isn't tied to your calendar invites or your performance reviews.

This is your season to reclaim authorship of your story and redesign your life so that it reflects the woman you are today. Not the woman who took that job 10 years ago. Not the girl who was just grateful to be chosen. But the woman who knows what she brings to the table and isn't afraid to build a new one.

When I first started to feel the early inklings of my desire to make a big life transition, I sat down to write a letter. That letter was to my future self. Well, come to think of it, it was more of a poetic profile, designing my future self. This was a version I knew I could become if I stopped seeking external approval and let go of fear and shame. I wasn't exactly sure how far into the future I would find this version of myself, but I knew in my heart exactly what she looked like and how she moved. She is a bona fide, unapologetic badass… period. She's got her shit together and stays focused on maintaining a level of grounded peace that cannot be disturbed by menial outside forces. She didn't just pop out of nowhere. She grew out of every challenge, every heartbreak, and every failure that taught her lessons necessary to navigate just about anything.

When I tell you I can see her so clearly, I mean it. I see her getting pissed off at me when I allow dumb stuff to get in the way of my personal development. I vividly see her rolling her eyes when I avoid doing the hard things, or when I start procrastinating like a child. I hear her decisive voice, whispering in my head when I try to hide my true, authentic self from the world. She yells at me when I outwardly proclaim I want to prioritize my health, but sit down to inhale another sugary pastry at one of my favorite coffee houses. In spite of her never-ending frustration with me constantly getting in my own way, she stays there, waiting patiently for me to do a little bit better each day. She keeps the light on, so I can find my way to her. She is the constant, gentle voice in my head, guiding me in the right direction so I am never confused along the path to reach her.

So what's in this letter? Take a look for yourself. It has remained a sweet private note that's never been seen by anyone else before I shared it in this passage. When I first put these words on paper, I posted them on the wall of my closet so I could see and read them out loud every morning as I dressed for the day. It was intentional so I would not forget or lose sight of the ultimate goal. To read these words each morning helped me remember who the fuck I was, before any outside elements tried to convince me otherwise. This note reminded me to show up and aim to be a little more like her, even in the smallest ways, until it became reality.

**Below is the design of my future self:**

*Show up as HER (until you become her).*

*You know her because she is you, but in the future, after you have figured out all your shit.*

*She knows her strength and doesn't seek anyone's approval to feel worthy.*

*Her presence leaves a mark.*

*She is the G.O.A.T. in every arena she enters.*

*She never plays small, but always remains grounded and grateful.*

*She finds joy in every new morning.*

*She doesn't waste time worrying about what's ahead, because what is within her is far greater, and always ready to move forward.*

*Her moves are strategic, steady, and efficient.*

*She does not have to overcome, because she intrinsically knows what is for her, and what is not worth her energy.*

*She is impatiently waiting for you to get over yourself and put in the work.*

*She did not grow into this by wishing for it. She worked for it. She made it happen.*

*She wants you to know your POWER.*

Each line holds a deeper meaning, containing words that trigger me into remembering individual elements that make up what I know I am capable of. I know every time I choose to make hard choices and do the work, I will grow into another layer of who I am meant to be. On that same note, I knew every time I avoided the tough, meaningful work, that all I was doing was slowing down the progress. That avoidance was delaying the transformation I knew I wanted. It was like taking the long, not-so-scenic, inconvenient, and more expensive route. The straight path was already laid out for me. Yeah, I *might* arrive at the same destination, but how much time and effort is wasted because I didn't follow the recommended directions in the first place? Plus, once I do get to my destination, how much regret will I bring with me because I took way too long avoiding the hard stuff? I knew all this because I was the architect of both the destination and the path to get there.

Since I first wrote those words, I'm happy to report that some of the elements have come into reality. My mindset is different now. The changes are deeper and not easily detected by the naked eye, but I guarantee I am getting closer. Some of my bucket list goals are on full display for you to witness. Sitting down to write this very book is one of my most deeply held personal goals. If you're reading this, I want to thank you for being part of my journey. Don't get it twisted. I haven't been sitting around doing absolutely nothing. I have run multiple marathons, gotten a doctoral degree, paid off massive personal debt, and lost weight numerous times. However, the fact that I can say I am finally a published author makes me more proud than I can adequately describe. My future self knew I could do this, and she is clapping for me right now.

So what about you? Have you designed your future self? If not, let's point out what is likely happening for you right now. There are some things I already know about you without the two of us ever having a conversation. You picked up this book for a reason. Your goals are a little abstract at the moment, but you already feel the discomfort of someone who is ready for a change. But exactly what that change is might be a bit foggy. You're looking around at parts of your life you held tightly for years, but now it feels like you've outgrown them a little. Things feel a little tight or bland. You are a person of faith and believe you should feel grateful for everything you have, but the guilt of wanting something different is unshakeable.

Let me give you some advice. That discomfort you are feeling is your future self giving you a nudge. She's trying to wake you up so you can begin to see her and recognize her. She is watching you go about your current routine and has decided it's time for you to begin this journey to come meet her. But the challenge is that in order to meet her, you are going to have to make a pivot. The path you are currently on is kind of circular, and keeps you rotating around the same things and the same mindset. You feel safe on the current path, because it is familiar, and you think you know what comes next.

The path you're on right now is paved with predictability. It's the well-worn route you've traveled for years, maybe decades. It knows your fears and feeds your routines. It doesn't challenge your potential because it was never meant to. But the version of you that's waiting on the other side of transformation? That version doesn't live at the end of the familiar road. They exist somewhere off the beaten path, where the terrain is uncertain and the light flickers with doubt, but the air is rich with possibility. You won't meet them by staying comfortable. You'll meet them by stretching beyond what feels safe, by saying yes to choices that feel just out of reach, and by trusting that if the challenge has arrived, it's because you already carry the strength to rise to it. That future version isn't waiting for you to be fully ready. They're waiting for you to just start.

Now that you've seen what this practice looked like for me, I want to offer you the space to do the same. Your version won't look exactly like mine. It's yours to design. You don't need to know every detail about the future or have complete clarity about what you want just yet. What matters is that you begin to imagine them. To picture the future version of yourself who is waiting on the other side of your pivot. They already know your strength, your softness, your brilliance. This next part is about starting to see them clearly and stepping toward that vision with intention. Let's begin.

### Meet Her: A Guided Visioning Activity for Your Future Self

Take a deep breath, friend.

Before we rush to define what's next, let's get still. You've just read about *my* future self. You know how I designed her, how she holds me accountable, how she reminds me daily who I'm becoming. Now it's your turn. Not to copy mine, but to create your own. To meet the version of yourself that already exists inside of you. She's not waiting for the "perfect timing." She's waiting for your *permission.*

Let's go find her.

### Step 1: Get Quiet. Get Real.

Find a space that feels safe and uninterrupted. Light a candle. Brew your favorite tea. Sit in a chair that hugs you back. This is sacred work, so treat it that way.

Close your eyes. Take a few deep breaths, and ask yourself:

- What version of me am I longing to meet?
- What does she feel like when she walks into a room?
- What has she let go of?

- What does peace look like in her body?

Let whatever images come, even if they feel distant or blurry. That's okay. We're not after perfection. We're making contact.

## Step 2: Start Describing Her

Now gently open your journal or a blank page. Begin to write out the details of this version of you. Not from the voice of who you are today, but from the voice of who you are becoming.

You might start with:

- "She wakes up in the morning and…"
- "Her days are filled with…"
- "She no longer tolerates…"
- "She is surrounded by…"

Be specific. Is she traveling more? Running her own business? Resting without guilt? Does she wear red lipstick or walk five miles every morning before sunrise? Let it all out. This is a portrait, not a resume.

## Step 3: Claim Her Power

Write down *how* she moves through life. What energy does she give off? What kind of boundaries does she hold? What kind of love does she accept? What kind of *truth* does she speak?

Examples might be:

- She leads with intention, not urgency.
- She doesn't second-guess her gut.
- She doesn't say "yes" when she means "no."
- She pours into others only after she's poured into herself.

These details matter. You're writing the emotional architecture of her life.

### Step 4: Write the Letter

Now that you've met her, it's time to talk to her.

Write a short letter to your future self. You can date it one year from today, or five. Speak to her with gratitude and curiosity. Ask her what you need to let go of. Tell her what you're committed to starting now so you can meet her sooner.

Here's a prompt to begin:

*Dear Future Me, I see you. I feel you. And I'm coming for you.*

Let her know you're not just hoping for her. You're building her, one decision, one boundary, one bold move at a time.

### Step 5: Post It Where You Can See It

Don't hide this. Place it somewhere you can return to when life starts to pull you off course. This can be a closet wall, your journal, the notes app on your phone, or even the bathroom mirror. This is not just a letter. It's a mirror. It's a compass. It's a promise.

You've just begun the most powerful part of your midlife pivot: *visioning without apology.*

Don't worry if you're not her yet. She's already within you. You're not starting from scratch. You're remembering. Every time you choose courage over comfort, truth over performance, presence over productivity, you step closer to her.

Now go write her into existence.

She's waiting.

# CHAPTER 2

## This Time, It's About Me

When I look back on photos of my elders, particularly my maternal grandmother, I see that her midlife years were very different from mine. As a matter of fact, I don't think she really had a midlife experience at all. Her life was filled with hard moments. By societal standards of her time, she likely had to speed from a shortened childhood, where she helped raise her younger siblings, into adulthood as a wife and mother to six children. Then she woke up one day as a grandmother. In my rough assumption, her life seemed to settle there for a bit.

Both she and my mom, who was the baby girl of my grandmother's children, had each reached marriage and motherhood by the time they were 20. By their 50s, both were grandmothers multiple times over and settled into retirement. Although their lives and careers followed their own separate paths, recognizing the parallels in those timelines always struck me. We lost my grandmother at 68 years old, which today feels so incredibly young. I didn't remember her that way, though. My memories of her were those of a traditional grandmother, one who kept her image safe in the "old lady" category. It wasn't until recent years that I heard more vivid stories about her that I was able to see the woman behind that matronly title.

I had the same revelation about my mother, too. She's still very much alive and living an active lifestyle, volunteering at her church with a broad group of close friends to share experiences with. When she divorced my father while I was in college, I harbored hard feelings for her decision. From my perspective, her leaving my dad broke up our family. It splintered our lives into jagged fragments. The recovery from that change was long and left some ugly scars. My resentment toward her decision lingered for years, but the Type A/good girl/rule follower in me did her best to follow along without saying anything that would make the situation worse.

My mom eventually remarried and has enjoyed a relatively comfortable life since. At the time, I only saw the shock and hurt the divorce caused. I saw how the breakup of my parents' marriage left lasting marks, and it angered me. This was the only perspective I could see for many years. My mom got her wish for a new life, and my dad got left behind. But this was from the narrow perspective of a child (I was 19 at the time), who no doubt could only see the parts that impacted a fairytale version of my childhood world.

Looking back, I can see the situation from a different perspective. Let me put all the proper math in place to fully understand this timeline. She married my dad at 18 years old and had me when she was 20. When my parents divorced, my mom was 39. Her midlife had basically started then. At that time, she had one kid in college (me) and one starting high school (my sister). She had been married 22 years and was done. All the reasons why the marriage ended are truths, settled somewhere between her and his perspectives, colored with emotions and blame. My dad was not without fault. Ultimately, she was opting for a new start and a different path for her midlife years. Of course, I did not see it that way at the time. However, now that I look back on that time from my own midlife vantage point, my view and judgment have softened significantly.

Technically, I would not classify age 39 as the true start of midlife. It seems a little young if you look at that number on paper. But if you scrutinize her life events that had already occurred by that time, you might agree that this was indeed a pivotal time for her. She wanted something different in life and took the gamble. I don't know what she would do differently if given the chance. Was the fallout worth it? Would you do it all again, knowing how it would impact the rest of us? It's a conversation we've never had. Just writing this passage has been more revealing than I am comfortable with, as far as this part of my life is concerned. But what I can say is that her decision was a bold one. She chose her own happiness first, and I choose not to fault her for that.

Any woman, especially black women, can attest to some pivotal moments where choosing our own happiness wasn't always an option. We haven't always been afforded time to choose softness and comfort. There was survival, and all the times we had to work to protect ourselves because no one else would. Our defenses have always been on high, because showing any element of vulnerability would not only get us hurt, but also regularly abused by a society that didn't see us as whole human beings deserving of love and care.

It sometimes angers me when I hear so-called compliments paid to the image of the strong black woman. To compliment black women as strong and resilient, lands backhandedly. We weren't strong because it was something we aspired to be. We were strong because we had to be. Systemically racist societal pressures have long held a knee to the neck of black women. While white women could exist in a place where their presence was revered and protected in chivalry, black women existed in a place where their presence was always under pressure. We have come to everyone else's rescue and held down the fort, as our men were beaten down and broken by this world. In their absence, for various reasons that were not always of their doing, we led the households without question because no one was coming to save us. We learned through generations of struggle that as black women, we had to save ourselves.

So when I hear about a woman of color choosing her own happiness and gliding toward a space where she can be soft or completely still, I cheer for her. I want that for all of us. For people of color, choosing joy and living it out loud is its own form of rebellion. Setting boundaries that protect that joy from outside interference is a flex. I see this with the younger generation, as they boldly take to social media and declare their embrace of the soft life, or give tips on living the life of a "lazy girl". They witnessed firsthand as the previous generations (us included) struggled and pushed aside our own dreams and desires, as if it were something we were supposed to do. This was sometimes because we had to, due to parental obligations and responsibilities. At other times, it was because we held on to outdated notions of virtue, assuming it was more righteous to put ourselves last on our own list of priorities.

We learned that putting others first and appearing selfless won us some unspoken prize that meant more points on the leaderboard of life. Initially, I rolled my eyes at this, but later had a change of heart when I realized these young folks were on to something. Holding tight to some virtuous ideals of self-sacrifice has been detrimental to our physical and mental health. But we charged on. Pushing through pain and exhaustion while sacrificing rest and recovery has cut our lifespans short. But we charged on. However, now I am here to deliver the message that it is okay to pivot away from this self-sacrificing mindset. You can choose yourself first and be selfish.

While we are on it, let's ditch the negative connotations that have been associated with that word, "selfish". The very definition of being selfish means you are putting yourself first. What's wrong with that? I embrace the word and the meaning when I describe my current outlook. I am selfish. My priorities are centered around what is best for me before I can begin to take on the well-being of everyone and everything else around me. The delicate care of my mental and physical health is now my first priority. Relentlessly pursuing joy and resting fully have allowed me to blossom into a version of myself that is pretty damn cool. It isn't complete yet either. This version of me is just beginning to evolve and shift as I hit midlife.

I felt it coming on when my kids started chasing their own independence. As they pulled away from my daily motherly support,

I felt the gap emerge between what they needed me to be and what I still wanted to become. Frankly, they didn't need me much anymore. Their friend circle was more influential than their parents once they hit their teenage years, and that is perfectly natural. But the first time they walk away out in the world without looking back, you have to take note of what you feel in that moment. It might be sadness and grief, as the innocence of their childhood comes to a close. It might be loneliness, because they leave you behind in exchange for their own social life, where you are not welcome. It is okay to acknowledge it for what it is. But I urge you not to stay in the grieving phase.

As parents, our main role is to raise our kids in a supportive, loving environment as best as we can. We spend their entire childhoods keeping them safe and worrying about whatever harms might cross their path that we need to prepare for. We teach them right from wrong, the importance of being a good person, and then send them out into the world in hopes that some of those lessons actually stick. So when the day comes when they are independent enough to no longer need us, that is a time to celebrate. You've accomplished the main objective of your parenting job, which is to raise your children to be independent, self-sufficient adults. So why do so many of us feel awful when our little birdies fly away from the nest?

Maybe it is the loss of no longer being the center of someone else's world. Perhaps it is the fear that all the lessons and things we taught them weren't enough. It could be even simpler than that. Maybe raising our kids was the center of our world, and when that is done, we don't know what to do with ourselves. So for some, we cling to our adult kids a little longer. We insert ourselves in their daily lives unprevoked. We provide an unconditional safety net that causes their independent growth to be stunted, instead of being developed. As a result, they continue to depend on that parental support and never stand on their own.

So let's go back to the early phase of empty nesting. You suddenly find yourself with newly grown kids who are trying on adulting for the first time, as if they are getting fitted for a new suit. It will take a few shopping trips and try-ons to find the right fit, but eventually, they will find the one. Let them. Allow them space to stumble through the process and figure some things out, without you hovering in the background. What if they mess that up, you ask? You should let them fail, and then be a listening ear when they talk through the situation and reflect. But most importantly, give them space to work through the failures. Let them learn from their own experience, and then again, as they try the next thing better. Their most impactful learning and development will come from doing.

From my own personal experience, I can definitely say my husband and I did our very best when it came to raising our kids and being ever-present as parents. That doesn't mean it was perfect. It wasn't. We had a mountain of challenges that we never seemed to be on the downside of. Frankly, there are still some elements of our relationship with my oldest son that we are still working through. When he hit his adolescent years, there were multiple identity crises he found himself at war with. He battled internally and with asshole peers, and then with others who humored him as he tried on various different personas in search of his true self. Instead of seeing mom and dad as his number one allies, he brought the battles home to us on a daily basis. We were easy targets because we were always there. He didn't see us as support, but instead as punching bags to take out his frustrations. We battled for years, right up until the day he moved out to start college.

Once he was settled in on campus, our entire household sighed with relief. We had done all we could as parents to get him safely and lovingly to this point of toe-dipping into independence. He eventually found a community of friends and was able to blossom into his own interests. Our relationship is delicate and clunky, but we are still working on it. My other son was starting his senior year of high school and graduating soon. So I dove in again, volunteering with all the parent committees and fundraising to help make his celebrations memorable. I had done the same with both boys and sprinted to the finish line of all the high school milestones with gusto.

I share all this because the reflection serves as a reminder that there is a season for all things. Nothing stays the same. Every season of life begins, blooms, and eventually fades. Parenthood is no different. When my kids were born, my husband and I dove into it as the most dedicated and responsible versions of ourselves. We gave everything to our roles as mom and dad. It didn't protect us from the challenges, but we knew we had done our best. I don't lie awake at night anymore wondering if we could have done anything differently, because I know we gave our all. Sure, we both grieve the rosy, happy outcomes that you see in the Hallmark movies, where whole families come home for the holidays to wear matching pajamas and sift through childhood home videos while sipping hot chocolate. Who knows if we'll ever get to that phase?

What I do know is that this empty nest season is an important one. There is suddenly a lot of open time on our calendars and in our daily routine. My evenings and weekends are wide open for me to do whatever I want. So what will that be? Do I even have a clue what I want to do? As a new empty nester, you now have the time and space to get reacquainted with this mature and wiser version of yourself. Ask yourself what you have thought about doing, but talked yourself out of, with the default assumption of not having time? How would you schedule your free time if you were able to be 100% selfish? Better yet, how would you spend this time without the guilt of being completely selfish?

**Dismantling the guilt of putting yourself first, for once.**

There was a time when I wore "selflessness" like a badge of honor. I spent a huge chunk of my career as an educator. So putting kids, especially other people's kids, first was central to the fabric of who I am. I poured into everyone, including my family, my job, and my community, until there was nothing left for me. I didn't rest unless everyone else was okay. I didn't dream unless it fit into someone else's schedule. Add to this that I certainly didn't ask for help, because I was too busy being the strong one. Also, with my own perfectionist tendencies constantly popping up, you get a better picture of how this compounds over time.

Sound familiar? Of course it does. That's because you've probably been this same person. Maybe the origins of this mindset are not your fault. Somewhere along the way, we were taught this. Good women, good mothers, good partners, good professionals, *good people*, sacrifice themselves. We learned to prioritize everyone else's needs while ours stayed buried under to-do lists, carpool schedules, staff meetings, and unspoken expectations of always showing up.

But here's the truth: Self-sacrifice isn't a virtue when it turns into self-erasure.

## Where the Guilt Comes From

This guilt, this nagging feeling that choosing yourself is somehow wrong, didn't come from nowhere.

It came from growing up in a culture that applauded women for being dependable, quiet, helpful, and available. We learned early that saying "yes" meant we were nice. We were told that putting ourselves first was selfish. All that ambition made us arrogant. Wanting rest was lazy. Being needed was a measure of our worth. Plus, we had the grand bonus of being liked by any and all who know us, regardless of whether we actually liked them in return. Being liked meant we were good, and being good felt like we had reached perfection.

Let's not pretend we only heard this in childhood. We've heard it in staff meetings and in church pews. It was spoken at family dinners. Sometimes it was even from our own inner voice, repeating outdated scripts we didn't realize we'd memorized.

But those rules? They were never designed to keep *us* whole. They were designed to keep us *useful*. And baby, you're more than just useful.

There is no other place in our adulthood where aiming to be perfect is more evident than in our careers. We are in constant competition and in comparison to our peers. Our output is measured. Our presence is monitored. Each time we deliver on our professional promises, our nervous system receives it like a dopamine hit. So we repeat the cycle again and again, sometimes with the reward, but many times without it. When that external validation isn't received, it doesn't stop the cycle. In fact, we internalize that it is our failure or our not measuring up that is to blame. So we push ourselves more and sacrifice our own needs in search of that validation from others.

This was definitely my story. Back in my educator days, I was a high school social studies teacher, and I truly loved it. My students came from low-income backgrounds, so I took it upon myself to make my classroom the most inviting place for them to experience new things that they might not have been exposed to otherwise. Bringing whole new experiences to them was something I internalized. If I didn't do this for them, who would? Like many teachers, that meant overspending my own money to supply them with the fundamentals. Because I worked at the high school level, that meant the start time was earlier than the other grade levels. The instructional schedule started around 7:15 am, so the overprepared perfectionist in me regularly arrived an hour before that. When classes ended around 3 pm, I overstayed until 5 pm or 6 pm to prepare for the next day.

That 12-hour schedule, which was mostly self-imposed, continued for all of my teaching years. No one asked me to do this. As a matter of fact, I don't think most of my colleagues even knew that I did it. I was normally one of the last cars in the parking lot when I left each day, so no one was around to even witness it. But I had some weird sense of self-righteousness every time I walked out of the building and realized I was the last one there. Surely this constant giving and sacrificing of my personal time meant I was a good and selfless person. That, in turn, meant I was better than my colleagues because I gave my all to these poor students who needed a hero to come to their rescue, right?

Let's fast forward to the burnout. It was a complicated burnout because of the fact that I mistakenly put the blame on my employer. I complained to my colleagues that *they* expect too much of us, that *they* make us work such long hours. But if I had done some honest reflection at the time, I would have remembered all the days when I put those expectations on myself. This changed a little when I hit motherhood, but not by much. I left work by a certain time because the daycare hours demanded it. I couldn't be late picking up my toddlers, or else I would be charged. Even then, I still took mounds of work home with me. As I spent most of my Sunday afternoons prepping with paperwork for the upcoming week, subconsciously, I knew there was no prize waiting for me when I got to work Monday morning. More work would be there, and I would place more invisible expectations on myself.

I was constantly putting myself last on my list of priorities, in exchange for the praise and admiration of people who had no obligation or care for what I was doing. I willingly did it to myself day after day, but directed the blame outwardly. Looking back, I now see I could have been far more efficient with my time. I could have volunteered a lot less for some team responsibilities. This would have given me back some time needed to plan my own lessons and give my students feedback on their work. I could have leaned into learning some technological hacks to automate a few tasks, so I would be freed up from taking baskets of student work home with me to grade over the weekends. I could have assigned less busy work for my students and spent more time really talking with them to better gauge the levels of progress.

I don't beat myself up over this realization. The younger, early-career version of myself did what she thought was best at that time. She was raised to work hard, be nice and likable, and not complain about it. Wanting or creating something different for yourself was seen as selfish, and selfish women were judged harshly. But why do some women still do it today, at this age, with all that we know?

Here's what I now know for sure. Working twice as hard for twice as long rarely gets you ahead of your workload. The work continues to be there, no matter how much you attack it. Plus, if you think anyone around you notices how much you put into your work, you would be wrong. It doesn't make them bad or horrible people. They have their own shit to worry about. Keeping up with your work progress or quality is not at the top of their list. Watching what time you come and go to work is also not their priority. As long as you carry your weight and deliver what you are tasked with, they won't notice much else. So, next time you are tempted to start pulling voluntary 12-hour shifts because you think it makes you look good, just don't. No one is watching, nor do they care. Leave the work there and come back the next day rested so you can fully contribute to the team.

Pulling all-nighters for work or for fun might have been cute when you were in your 20s or 30s, but not anymore. Rest is now the ultimate flex. Your work goals must shift to focus on all the ways you can be the most efficient with your daily tasks, enabling you to complete what needs to be done within the allotted work hours. Consistently working extended hours is so 1990s, so we need to leave that behind, just like we left behind those stiff LottaBody sista-curl hairdos, too.

**The Cost of Putting Yourself Last**

Let's talk about what all this selflessness has cost us.

- Dreams deferred until "the kids are older" or "the timing's right."

- Exhaustion that runs so deep, even a vacation doesn't fix it.

- Resentment is bubbling under the surface because no one notices all we do, and we're too tired to keep doing it.

- A career path that once lit you up but now feels like a prison you can't admit you've outgrown.

That kind of burnout doesn't just happen overnight. It creeps in, in the name of love, loyalty, and duty. Before you know it, you're the reliable one. The fixer. The go-to. The strong one who never gets to be soft.

But here's what I need you to know: Choosing yourself isn't betrayal. It's restoration.

**Flipping the Script**

There's power in saying: *This time, it's about me.*

It's not because you don't care about others, but because you've finally realized that pouring from an empty cup helps no one. What if putting yourself first wasn't selfish, but sacred? What if your joy, your rest, your dreams, your voice... actually mattered? Not in theory. Not "when the kids are grown." Not "after things calm down." But right now.

Here's your permission slip to stop explaining your "no." Here's your reminder that peace is a valid priority. Here's your invitation to make yourself the main character in your own life story. Because if not now, when?

**Strategies to Center Yourself Without Apology**

Let's get practical. Here are a few ways to start shifting your life from default mode to *intentional self-prioritization*:

**1. Create a "ME First" Filter**

Before you say yes to anything, whether it's a meeting, a favor, or a new responsibility, you need to ask yourself a few questions:

- Does this align with the version of me I'm becoming?
- Will this drain or energize me?
- Is this a *yes* out of guilt, fear, or obligation?

If the answer is "yes, but I'll resent it later," then it's a *no* now.

**2. Schedule Yourself First**

Treat your self-care like you treat other people's emergencies. Put it on the calendar and honor it. Rest, workouts, solitude, journaling, lunch with a friend, or whatever fills your cup, goes on the schedule *before* the world fills it for you.

**3. Use Boundaries as Your New Love Language**

Try these phrases:

- "That doesn't work for me right now."
- "I'm not available, but thanks for thinking of me."
- "Let me get back to you after I check in with myself."

These are not rude. These are revolutionary.

**Still Feeling Guilty?**

You're not alone. But let me say this gently: Your guilt is not your GPS. It's just a signal that you're doing something new and bold. It is something that disrupts a pattern you've outgrown.

Remember:

- You are allowed to outgrow roles you once prayed for.

- You are allowed to want ease.

- You are allowed to take up space.

Here's a journal prompt: What would I do if I weren't afraid of disappointing anyone?

Write it out. Sit with it. That answer? That's your next clue.

## Reclaiming the Narrative

Midlife is not about shrinking to fit the expectations of others. It's about expanding into your own becoming. Self-prioritization isn't a rejection of others. It's a reconnection to yourself. And when you show up as your whole self, everyone benefits. Your energy shifts. Your decisions change. Your peace becomes non-negotiable.

Repeat after me:

*I don't have to earn rest.*

*I don't need permission to evolve.*

*I am allowed to make myself the priority.*

This time, it's about *you.* And you're worth it.

## Recovering Good Girl

You often hear about folks, women in particular, who spend the better part of their lives doing the people-pleasing dance. You know the one: going above and beyond for everyone else, always showing up, always being the dependable one, often to your own detriment. It's the art of self-sacrifice disguised as virtue. You do it in the hope that your goodness, your helpfulness, your reliability, will earn you favor. That someone will look at you and say, "Now that's someone I want around." We might not even realize we're auditioning for acceptance. We just call it being "nice," or "doing what's right."

Somewhere in our childhood, the seeds are planted. Maybe it's when we got our first gold star for being quiet in class or the praise for letting someone else have the last cookie. We saw the way adults lit up when we were agreeable and compliant. So we kept at it. Over time, that simple cause-and-effect loop, good behavior equals approval, becomes hardwired.

By the time we hit middle school or high school, the groups are already forming. Some of us naturally fall into the right cliques, but others have to squint and contort ourselves into the shape that's "liked." That's when the performance begins. It's subtle at first. You start changing how you laugh, pretending to like the same music, biting your tongue instead of speaking your mind. That's your "pick me" era. When it works and you're picked, or let into the circle, it feels warm and validating. It feels like belonging.

But here's the trap: if you have to perform to belong, you never really feel safe taking off the mask.

I wore my "good girl" mask like it was stitched to my skin. I wasn't just a rule follower; I was the rule enforcer. I got the grades, earned the accolades, and racked up praise like trophies. My self-worth was tethered to gold stars and glowing evaluations. It wasn't just that I liked being good; I needed to be seen as good. My value was tied to being liked, appreciated, and applauded.

Looking back now, I can see how much I craved external validation. I'd over-prepare, over-deliver, and still ask, "Was that okay?" The thing is, when the dopamine hit from praise wears off, you're left with a hollow ache. You realize you've built a life according to someone else's blueprint.

I remember finishing my doctoral degree, which was a monumental accomplishment by any measure. But within days, a whisper crept in: "Was that even worth it?" The applause had barely died down, and I was already questioning whether it was my dream I'd been chasing or someone else's.

In my career, I climbed steadily, quietly, efficiently. I took on the hard projects, played the politics carefully, and rarely ruffled feathers. I did what good girls do. I made myself indispensable without ever really asking what I wanted. When I finally decided to pivot in my career after more than twenty years, I realized I had overstayed my best years in a role that no longer felt aligned. Yet I stayed because it looked good. Because it earned me admiration. Because it was safe.

So, fast-forward to these midlife years, when I can now look back at all the "safe" choices I made (career, education, even how I moved through the world) and realize how much of it was about staying inside a bubble of comfort and praise. It was built mostly by not rocking the boat. Let me tell you, that bubble eventually started to feel less like safety and more like suffocation.

Here's a question for you. I mean this in the most loving, non-judgmental way: When was the last time you made a decision purely because it felt *right* to you? Not because it made sense on paper. Not because it would look good on your résumé or please the people around you. But because your spirit whispered, "Yes. This."

If you're struggling to come up with an answer, I want you to know, you're not alone. I went years making choices that made other people proud of me, but left me unsure if I even recognized myself anymore. I wasn't unhappy, necessarily. But I was disconnected and out of sync with the woman I knew I could be if I gave myself permission to stop performing.

Midlife has a funny way of revealing the quiet truths we've pushed aside for decades. It doesn't always show up as a dramatic breakdown. It can be a subtle tug, a growing awareness that you want something different, deeper, more honest.

This isn't about blaming anyone. Society handed us the script, but we turned the pages, and that's okay. The good girl version of us helped us survive. She got us through the expectations, the degrees, the promotions, and the busy seasons of life. But now? We don't owe her forever.

This is where the recovery begins. It's not about swinging to the opposite extreme or throwing out everything you've built. It's about pausing and asking better questions. We can try being more honest. Try saying 'no' when you mean 'no'. Test drive choosing yourself even when it's uncomfortable. When my dear friend and author, Dr. Shanaya Anderson, visited the podcast to share her expertise on introverted women in leadership roles, she touched on a very simple lesson so many of us could benefit from right away. She says one common mistake we make in midlife is stressing about things that are beyond our control, and not taking advantage of the areas that are fully within our control. The stress comes from wasting energy, pushing against the immovable wall of things we cannot change. Instead, she urges us to take a step back and evaluate where we do have control and start from there.

Changes that are within your control don't need a permission slip. You don't need anyone else's applause to validate your next move. Most of all, you don't have to perform to be loved. You just have to show up, real, imperfect, and present. If nobody has told you this lately, let me say it clearly: The woman you're becoming is already enough, and I'm rooting for her.

## The Turn Toward Yourself

So now what?

Now that we've pulled off the mask, acknowledged the years spent performing, and given our inner "good girl" a soft place to rest, what comes next?

This is the part where things shift. Where the focus begins to turn inward. Where all the time, energy, and emotional labor we once poured into everyone else begins to be redirected toward ourselves. That idea can feel unsettling at first. For many of us, especially those raised to prioritize others, choosing ourselves feels unnatural, maybe even selfish.

By midlife, we've often worn a dozen different hats. We've been caretakers, professionals, partners, parents, and volunteers. We've shown up, held it down, and kept things together. Sometimes with joy, often with exhaustion, and more often than we like to admit, with a quiet sense of sacrifice. All of it mattered. All of it shaped us. Still, we arrive at this point in life with a hauntingly honest question: what's left for me?

This isn't a question rooted in regret. It's a question that opens the door to possibility. There are dreams that have waited patiently for us to circle back. Goals that were shelved because the timing wasn't right, or we didn't believe we were ready, or we thought we had more time. Now, with more years behind us than ahead, the urgency to honor those dreams begins to grow.

For many women, midlife can feel like standing at a crossroad. We are often more aware of time. We reflect more deeply. We long for meaning and clarity. The old markers of success begin to feel insufficient, and we yearn for something that feels personal and real.

This is where I want to challenge you. Do not let your dreams go to the grave with you. Do not let your goals die inside your journals or your someday list. Give some real consideration to the business idea, the book, the degree, the career shift, the house by the water, the solo trip abroad, or whatever has been living quietly in the corners of your heart. It still matters.

Too many of us have been conditioned to wait for the perfect time. We wait until the kids are grown, the debt is paid, the schedule clears, or the stars align. The truth is, perfect timing is a myth. Life rarely slows down long enough for us to catch up unless we claim that space intentionally.

You have already proven that you can show up for others. Now it is time to show up for yourself. Don't only think about this in theory. You are not pushing it to someday. Start looking at now.

Your dreams are not too big. Your desires are not too late. Your goals have not expired. They are yours. They are still alive because there is still time.

You are not starting over. You are beginning again, equipped with wisdom, strength, and a sense of self that only midlife can offer. This is your invitation to live forward, on purpose.

Your next chapter is waiting.

# CHAPTER 3

## When the Job No Longer Fits the Woman: Career pivots for midlifers who've outgrown roles they once prayed for

There's a moment you'll reach in your career where the title, the paycheck, and the responsibilities that once made you proud now feel like a tight suit you've outgrown. You've evolved, but the role hasn't. Now, showing up every day feels like you're playing a character in someone else's story.

This chapter is for the woman who's waking up and wondering, "What happened to the version of me I used to be excited about?"

For me, my executive role in education was everything I had ever worked for, and every box was checked. The title was impressive, the salary generous, and the benefits sufficient. Plus, I had the satisfaction of hearing my parents tell their friends that they didn't know exactly what I did, but they knew I was "pretty close to the top" on my leadership level. To everyone around me, it looked perfect. Honestly, for a while, it felt perfect. Until one day, I walked into the office, sat at my beautifully organized desk in my spacious corner office with floor-to-ceiling windows, and felt utterly disconnected from it all.

That feeling wasn't new, but I'd been pushing it aside, buried beneath layers of busywork and professional obligations. However, now, here it was, unmistakably clear. The "perfect" job no longer matched who I had become. It was an outfit I had outgrown, stylish yet stifling, and tailored for someone I no longer recognized.

I wrestled with guilt. How dare I feel this way when I had so much? I grappled with fear, imagining the looks I'd receive when I walked away from something "so good." Then there was shame. Why wasn't I grateful enough? These emotions were heavy, tangled knots that kept me awake night after night.

When I went into my education role and finally reached the executive level, I had checked all the boxes, earned all the credentials, and hit every milestone. I expected to feel fulfilled. I had done everything right. However, instead, I felt the quiet ache of misalignment. That was the moment I knew something had to shift.

Let me say this. I wasn't one of those people who hated the work. In fact, I was proud of what I accomplished during that season. I wasn't chasing a trend or trying to jump ship for the sake of it. I had done good work. I had made an impact. However, I also realized that I was still young enough to make an impact somewhere else. I was capable enough to rebuild myself in a new space if I chose to. That didn't mean I had all the answers. I most certainly did not.

I still had doubts and continued to run mental loops full of "what ifs." Yet even in the uncertainty, something started stirring. It was a curiosity. I became curious enough to wonder: What else is out there for me? How else can I contribute? What might this next chapter look like?

With that curiosity came discomfort, restlessness, and a bit of anxiety. I started to feel the itch, to reach out, to explore, to try something different. I began questioning everything I thought I knew about success, stability, and what a "good life" was supposed to look like.

Curiosity alone isn't always enough. Sometimes, we stay right where we are, not because we're content, but because we simply don't know how to make the leap. The desire for something different burns quietly under the surface, but without a clear path forward, it feels safer to stay put. That is a fear of the unknown, of starting over, and of not having a roadmap. That's what holds so many of us in place. It's not a lack of ambition; it's a lack of guidance. According to Caroline Castrillon in *Forbes* (2023), some of the most common fears around career change in midlife include financial instability, fear of failure, and identity loss. Yet acknowledging these fears is the first step in navigating past them. When we name what scares us, we're better equipped to take strategic action instead of staying frozen in place.

When I began informing people about my intention to make a change, reactions ranged from shock to disappointment. I had built deep, meaningful relationships during my tenure in education, and I understood their reactions. However, I realized this decision was for me. I had reached a point where being selfish was necessary. My decision was either choosing their comfort or my own growth. I chose me.

Unexpectedly, after the initial shock wore off, many started asking specific questions about how I was navigating this transition. These weren't critical or judgmental questions; they came from genuine curiosity. They, too, had been feeling discontent, uncertain about their next steps, and lacked someone they could openly discuss these vulnerable career-shifting questions with. The fear and complexity of the unknown forced them back to their familiar routines.

You see, working in education is special. There are moments when you truly feel you are doing the Lord's work. We use terms like being an educator is a "calling", and it is not hard work, but "heart" work. Those words can bring comfort from time to time, but the reality is that it is still a job. No matter how noble the work is, you are still paid in exchange for your time and expertise. When you decide you no longer want to do that job, you should be allowed to make a shift without shame or judgment. It took me a while to find my voice and use the words that articulated what I was feeling. But when I did finally ease into it, I found there were several of my peers who were eager to listen.

It was in these heartfelt conversations that I recognized a new purpose emerging. There's a quote I once heard from Rory Vaden: "You are most powerfully positioned to serve the person you once were." This quote resonated so deeply and guided my decision to help others navigate similar transitions. Who could have guessed that I would find a new career path in my own struggle to figure out my own?

I found joy and purpose in being a guide, helping midlife professionals understand how to pivot effectively, what steps to take, and what unnecessary fears to release. Witnessing others transform their uncertainty into clear action has been profoundly rewarding. It doesn't guarantee perfection or effortless transitions. But it does demand clarity, purpose, and intentional steps.

Ultimately, the job didn't change; I did. That realization was empowering. Midlife, I've learned, is precisely the moment when we reassess and recalibrate. It's an invitation, not to reject what we've built but to realign with who we are now.

Taking steps away from that role wasn't easy. It required deep introspection, open conversations, and courage. However, when I finally let it go, the relief was immediate and profound. It opened doors I hadn't considered, revealing a landscape rich with possibilities better aligned with my values, dreams, and joy.

If you're sitting at a desk, in a job, or in a life that feels tight around the edges, take a moment. Pause. Reflect. Trust that inner voice nudging you toward alignment. The perfect job is one that evolves with you, not one you shrink yourself to fit.

**You Outgrew What You Once Prayed For**

Many of us spent the early years of our careers hustling for roles we thought would define us. We prayed for that job offer, clung to job security like it was the prize, and convinced ourselves that stability was the reward. For that season, it was all good. But midlife isn't about surviving. It's about aligning.

When the job no longer fits the woman, it's not a failure; it's a signal. It is a holy nudge and a gut whisper that it's time to make room for who you've become and what you now need. That kind of shift requires courage.

You see, many of us were raised with a certain blueprint: you find a good job, preferably one with benefits, and you hold onto it. You show up, you work hard, and you give your all. You're dedicated, loyal, and grateful. At the end of your years, you're supposed to waltz gracefully into retirement, with a pension and a party, after staying with the same employer for two or three decades. I saw this in my parents, who diligently dedicated their working lives to stable jobs. I admired their steadfastness and internalized their values deeply.

However, that story has shifted. The landscape has changed. That promise of loyalty being rewarded with stability and security? It's no longer the norm. Heck, these days it is downright rare. Now, staying in a job for decades doesn't guarantee safety or satisfaction. Many of my peers discovered new heights in their careers precisely by changing roles every few years, growing their skills, and negotiating better pay with more satisfying opportunities.

For many of us in midlife, we're waking up to the realization that clinging to that old narrative may actually be keeping us stuck. Can you recall moments when loyalty kept you from pursuing exciting opportunities? Have you ever felt tethered by expectations set by previous generations? A feature in the *Relational Psych* by Dr. Carly Claney (2024) found that more professionals over 50 are leaving behind roles that once defined them in order to seek fulfillment and alignment. Most of them don't regret the decision, even when it required a temporary step down in salary or prestige. This is because they finally felt like they were living more authentically.

We come from families where longevity in a single job or industry was seen as honorable. Our parents and grandparents worked in plants, post offices, school districts, or factories for thirty or forty years. In return, they were taken care of. That was the deal. However, that deal doesn't exist anymore.

## My amateur attempt to negotiate a pay raise

I need to add some context to my exit from my education career. It wasn't just a curiosity for something new that propelled me. It was also an embarrassing wake-up call that I was being played. I discovered that a colleague in a similar position with equal credentials, less seniority, and fewer direct reports was earning significantly more than I was. I'm talking about way more. Plus, this person was slated to receive another title and pay bump when the new contract year began. I also learned that other new colleagues at my level had been recruited at my same salary, even though I had more seniority and had been promoted a few times to reach my salary level.

How did I know this? A lot of the information came directly from those individuals, because people are remarkably forthcoming with financial details when you know what to listen for. Some also came from my immediate supervisor, who was apparently proud of the changes that were happening. Maybe my supervisor wasn't aware of the fact that I made well below this colleague, or barely equal to my less senior colleagues. Maybe he didn't think I deserved that equal pay. Maybe it was an honest oversight. Maybe he didn't care. I didn't know for sure.

What I did know was that if anything was to be done about it, it would require me to first speak up and draw attention to the matter. I gathered the nerve to schedule a meeting with my boss to express my concerns. Naively, I didn't prepare anything…no documents, no supporting data. I planned to speak to the heart of what I was feeling and would lean on the fact that I had been with the organization for 23 years. My loyalty and dedication to the organization had to mean something, right? I was talented enough and well-liked with a solid reputation. I could have left to go work for another organization years ago, but I chose to stay. That meant something, too, right? Surely they would sense my unhappiness and would move quickly to appease me in hopes I would stay and continue to be their shining star. I was that important and valued, right?

The day came to meet with him. I stated my case as planned. He listened and appeared to thoughtfully consider what I said. To his credit, he likely didn't have much power over my exact pay, since a lot of that decision-making was centralized in the HR department, which is where he directed me next. Another meeting with the HR chief was scheduled. At that meeting, I was indeed offered a pay increase, but it was still well below what this colleague and other newer colleagues were being paid. I was crushed when he told me this was their "best and final offer".

I was told to think it over before signing my renewal contract, so I took the next few weeks to agonize over this offer versus another offer from a new organization. To be completely honest, the new company had not been a serious consideration before this letdown. I was fully expecting this process of getting the pay I felt I deserved to be more of a formality. Getting what I wanted was the only outcome I envisioned. I never expected to lose, so to speak. There should have been shockwaves felt throughout the organization, as I, one of the golden girls, had expressed discontent, and they would scramble to make their best efforts to keep me happy and avoid any risk of losing me. Boy, was I living in a delusional fantasy.

After some deliberation with the hubby, I kept my promise to my boss that I would let him know what my final decision was first before responding to HR's official offer. I sat across from him in his office when I shared that I had decided to turn down the offer. Embarrassingly, in a moment when I should have felt some inkling of satisfaction from his shocked reaction, I started to cry. Ugh! Getting overwhelmed with emotion and allowing the stupid tears to flow made me feel like I had rolled over and revealed a dumb bluff. It should have been a triumphant moment. I should have been able to deliver this blow and walk out of his office feeling like I had the last laugh. Instead, I felt like someone who had begged to be liked and got shot down.

Ultimately, I accepted the other company's job offer, which turned out to be for less pay than I had initially expected in the long run. Yes, I was doing something new. I learned a lot of new skills and got to experience a whole new work environment and culture. However, had I stayed and accepted the puny pay bump that was originally offered to me at my old job, it would have been for the same pay, ironically.

So did I regret leaving? No, because I really had outgrown the work I was doing. The problem was that my career path was quite narrow where I was. The only advancement was for roles that I no longer wanted. The only growth was in accepting more responsibilities for a very small pay increase. There wouldn't be any additional big promotions for someone who was already operating at the executive level. I loved my team and felt proud of what we had accomplished in the past, but most days, I was sleepwalking through the work. In this organization, my biggest challenges were behind me. My choices were to stay and count my days until early retirement eligibility or leave to find something in a completely new field.

Obviously, I chose the latter, and the whole transition experience opened my eyes to so many things. For one, I learned that I, as an individual, wasn't special. Although my ego was quite bruised in the aftermath, understanding how easily my organization was willing to part ways helped me understand that I was just one small piece of a much larger puzzle for them. I was replaceable. My work really could be done by someone else, and probably for much less money than what I was asking for. Ultimately, for them, that was a win.

Secondly, I had held on to the ridiculous notion that my seniority and loyalty to the organization offered me some sort of status, or at least protection, from any unwanted outcomes. I worked in the K12 education space, so this was a widely held assumption among educators. There are many who believe in the idea of joining the education world as if it were a lifelong oath of service. If you stay loyal, you'll be rewarded with protection and love, and eventually an easy, peaceful retirement. However, I had witnessed how quickly those long-time workers were forgotten, as their desk chairs and other items were swiped from their office as soon as the breakroom-retirement-party-cake had been served. Why should I have ever thought my situation would be different?

Another huge lesson learned was that I had failed to prove my value. I made big, incorrect assumptions that my boss and the larger organization somehow understood how hard I worked and what my team and I had accomplished. When the time came for me to state my case for a pay raise, I provided no data to prove what I had done for the organization. There was no tracking of improvements that were made possible by my big projects. There were no artifacts to illustrate my impact. There were no testimonials to help tell my story. There was only me, crying like a fool in front of my boss in a moment of utter defeat.

At that time, I was barely 48. I wasn't yet dreaming of walking off into the retirement sunset. There were still skills I wanted to learn and talents I wanted to use. There had always been an idea that I would move on to something different eventually, but frankly, it was just that…an idea. No real plan or actions had ever been considered to make this happen. It was something I would say out loud in a moment of frustration, or when I was talking big shit in front of an audience. Had I researched any job opportunities? No. Had I given serious thought to what I wanted to do when I moved on from my K12 role? No. Had I even reached beyond my little professional bubble to meet new people or get real insights about what I might be qualified for? No again.

Why hadn't I done any of this? I was scared, plain and simple. Although I was a golden girl in that environment, the possibility that I might not be as talented or skilled as I thought, and therefore not successful elsewhere, was a very clear and present insecurity. My pay might have been the catalyst to throw myself into this rabbit hole, but it wasn't bad. It was lower pay than what I thought I was worth in comparison to what my colleagues were already receiving. It was comfortable, but I truly had no clue what I was qualified to do or what the market rate was for whatever my talents and skills were. It was like I was a 22-year-old college grad all over again, trying to figure out what I wanted to do for a living. To be honest, I had no real clue how to figure this out.

By all outward appearances, my school district colleagues perceived my leaving as some huge uplevel, moving on to bigger and better things. To them, I was breaking through the bubble and into a space of mythical unknowns. As the story circulated about my pending departure, I moved around with a false bravado, allowing my colleagues to believe that narrative. In truth, I was just accepting the only job offer that was on the table. It was something I had not looked for. A former professional connection was leaving her job and asked if I'd be interested in applying to be her replacement. There was no big search process, and no competition that made me the victor. All in all, it was something that landed in my lap, and I never questioned it or vetted it much further. When I decided to leave my K12 job in a bit of haste, it was the only option I had to keep me from crawling back into my current comfort zone and continuing the status quo.

Counting down the years until my teacher retirement eligibility felt like a slow death, so I chose the alternative. Although this new job prospect wasn't what I really planned for, I knew deep down that it was the first step that could lead me to what I ultimately wanted. So the job offer was accepted a little blindly, with me not truly understanding what to question or what to expect. They offered, I said yes, and with no negotiations or friction.

One question lingered. Who would I be when I left my executive title behind? Without that status, how would I move forward? Dr. Claney states that imposter syndrome for midlifers is real, as they navigate away from a familiar career and into a new field. There is a fear of failure, because that fear of not succeeding outweighs the potential for growth.

The position I held and my education credentials bought me status in this world. It was respected. People took notice when I entered a space. They would defer to me when a big decision needed to be made. The realization that this would not follow me into my new role sent me into a full-blown identity crisis that caught me off guard. It took years and hard work to earn that respect, but I was willingly stripping myself of it. It was my armour, and my protection. I was a walking billboard for my organization. My movement, my current and future activities revolved around consideration for this organization. All my professional memories, connections, and accomplishments were earned within that bubble. Without that insulation, who or what was I?

## The Emotional Wear-and-Tear of Staying Too Long

Staying in a job that no longer serves you does something subtle but dangerous: it chips away at your confidence and convinces you that discomfort is just "part of adulting." But we weren't made to settle for dread. Not at this stage in the game. Research findings from the *Relational Psych Group* (2023) emphasize that chronic dissatisfaction in your professional life doesn't just lead to burnout.

It also dulls your creativity, sense of purpose, and even your ability to envision a different path forward. Rediscovering your passion often requires stepping away from a role that no longer reflects who you are becoming.

If you're experiencing burnout, resentment, or invisibility, those aren't flaws. They're flags. They're telling you: something no longer fits.

## Midlife Pivots Aren't About Starting Over. They're About Realigning

Too many women fear that changing careers at 45, 50, or beyond means starting from scratch. But here's the truth: you are not starting over. You're starting from experience. Robert Annis shared about the concept of having a portfolio career in his article for LinkedIn (2024). This is where professionals in midlife are combining multiple interests, part-time roles, or consulting gigs to build meaningful second acts. These transitions aren't about abandoning old skills. They're about remixing them into something new and self-defined.

When I first heard the term "portfolio career", it hit me immediately as a spot-on description of my current career status. Even today, I struggle to accurately form a cohesive response when someone asks what I do for a living. You see, as I built my modest coaching business, I held on to my full-time corporate job. At that same time, I also launched my YouTube channel and wrote my first book. Each of these brought in income, and I was passionate about them all. Depending on the time of day, whichever one I was working on held my undivided attention. I will proudly sit next to you at a dinner party and blab on and on about what I do, but it may never again fit into one nice, neat box.

The same can be true for you. Your transferable skills, leadership maturity, conflict resolution, deep listening, strategic thinking, and empathy are all premium assets. You just need to know how to repackage them for the next chapter. I would bet you probably do these things for friends and colleagues outside regular work hours already. You do some things with ease that others may struggle with. You do for free what others might be willing to pay for as a service. Do I have your attention yet?

This is why I coach midlifers through my career transitions program, not to start from zero, but to repurpose the power they already hold. You may have all the talent and know-how to start making money on the side without breaking a sweat.

## Use Your Network. Don't Start From Scratch

As I said on the podcast, "Who you know is just as important as what you know." You're not trying to hustle your way into rooms where no one knows your name. The truth is, someone you already know could unlock the next opportunity. But they won't think of you if you're silent, stuck, or playing small. So we do the scary thing. We speak up. We reach out. We tell people what we're moving toward, and we let them help us get there.

## Reflection: When the Role No Longer Fits

Midlife often reveals a quiet truth we've been trying to ignore: the role we once worked so hard to grow into no longer fits the version of us we are becoming. This is not a failure. It's an awakening. This chapter explored what it feels like to outgrow a role, a title, or even an entire career path. Now, let's turn inward.

This isn't about rushing into the next thing. It's about honoring the signals your body, spirit, and instincts have been whispering to you. Use these prompts to help surface what's been stirring under the surface.

## 1. The Honest Truth

Take a moment and reflect. Which of these statements feels true for you? Rather than checking a box, respond in a sentence or two about how it shows up in your daily experience.

- *"I dread Mondays more than I enjoy Fridays."*

- *"I feel invisible or undervalued at work."*

- *"My role doesn't reflect my full skill set anymore."*

- *"I've fantasized about quitting, even without a backup plan."*

- *"I'm playing small to avoid conflict or disappointment."*

- *"I've grown, but my job responsibilities haven't."*

What came up for you as you considered these truths?

## 2. A Moment of Clarity

Think back to a moment, big or small, when it hit you: *"This job, this title, this version of work is no longer aligned with who I am."*

- What happened?

- How did it make you feel?

- What did you *wish* you could have said or done at that moment?

## 3. What's Emerging in You Now?

As one chapter of your work identity winds down, another is preparing to unfold. Let's listen to that inner whisper.

- What are you curious about lately, even if it seems random or impractical?

- What kinds of challenges or problems feel exciting to solve?

- What kind of work lights you up, even if you're not "qualified" yet?

- What would your ideal day of work *feel* like, emotionally, creatively, spiritually?

Write freely here. Let go of expectations and titles. This is just for you.

## 4. Transfer Your Power

You are not starting from scratch. You are starting from *experience*.

Create a list that maps your current responsibilities or life experience to the skills they've helped you build. Then, imagine how those same skills might show up in a completely different context, even in your own business or side hustle.

## Example:

- *Current Task:* Planning team events
- *Transferable Skills:* Organization, Vendor Coordination, Budgeting
- *Possible Side Hustle:* Event planning, travel coordination, virtual assistant services Now it's your turn.
- What have people often come to you for help with?
- What do you enjoy doing that others find difficult?
- Are there talents you've downplayed because they've never been attached to a formal job title?

## 5. Start Where You Are: Your Hidden Hustle Potential

Don't underestimate the quiet brilliance of your everyday skills.

You may already have the foundation for a side hustle that brings in extra income, without needing another degree or a complicated business plan. Think about this:

- Have you helped someone edit their resume or prepare for an interview?

- Do you make amazing meals, crafts, or content that people ask about?

- Have you led workshops, planned events, organized spaces, or mentored others?

Now ask yourself: *If someone handed me $100 to teach, create, or organize something this weekend, what would I feel confident doing?*

Write it down. Explore it. Even a tiny experiment can spark big momentum.

**Final Prompt:**

What's one small, bold step you're willing to take this week to honor what you've discovered in this reflection?

Maybe it's researching a new interest, talking to a friend about your idea, or blocking off one hour to brainstorm possibilities.

Write it down. Then take that step. Your future self is counting on you.

# CHAPTER 4

## You Better Keep Those Receipts:
## Documenting Your Greatness Because
## Silence Won't Get You Seen

There's a moment in every midlife professional's journey when you realize: *you've done the work, but no one remembers but you*. Sometimes, not even you.

You've shown up early. Stayed late. Solved the crisis. Rewrote the strategy. You coached the new hire. Balanced budgets and people's egos. Without knowing every detail of your professional journey, I also know without a doubt that you sacrificed your own well-being in order to give your last ounce of energy and sanity to your job. But when it's time to talk about your impact in interviews or performance reviews, you draw a blank. You feel a little overwhelmed just thinking about starting over and competing in a space where you could teach a masterclass on every aspect of it. You gave the job everything, and somehow, you are left with no proof.

That stops now. Grab your pen and paper, or open up your notes app, because class is now in session. You might also need whatever beverage of choice that puts you in a productive mood, because this will take a while and some deep thought. I personally work best with an iced caramel latte ready for me to sip, but you do you. Ready, my dear? Let's get started.

"You better keep those receipts" isn't just catchy advice. It's a midlife career strategy. My favorite bit of advice for midlife professionals is to "collect your receipts". Why? Think of it in the literal sense. When you make a purchase, you get a receipt as evidence of the transaction. If you need to return the item, you'll present proof of what you paid (i.e., the receipt).

The same goes for your career accomplishments. When you want to defend your exceptional past work performance, you'll need to provide evidence. Your resume is only part of this. The rest is in the form of portfolio work samples, certificates, awards, and project accolades (i.e., receipts).

Don't expect anyone else to remember your professional contributions. That's YOUR responsibility. But when it is time to showcase your value, you'll have the "receipts". See how that works?

If you've felt overlooked or invisible in your workspace, this lesson is definitely for you. As a Gen X professional, you likely grew up being taught by your Baby Boomer parents that hard work pays off. You were expected to put your head down and do the work longer and harder than everyone else. Then you would be rewarded with care and loyalty from your employer. You probably also believed that your seniority within any organization earned you a bit of clout and respect among your peers. Deep down, you believed your supervisors recognized your undying dedication to your performance and would speak up for you in moments when it mattered. If there were ever cuts or layoffs, you just knew that you were so critical to their operation that you would be spared from any job loss.

Let me virtually hold your hand while you read this. None of that matters. More specifically, it doesn't matter if you cannot prove it. No, they didn't see you work those extra-long, unpaid hours. No, they didn't watch you carry home loads of work to finish over the weekend. No, they aren't aware of how many days you showed up to work sick, sleep-deprived, or mentally spent for the sake of keeping the department afloat.

But let's clarify first. These moments are not the receipts you need to keep. Those moments are just symptomatic of a mindset that led you to believe in a workplace fairytale. As a member of that professional organization, you are paid money in exchange for the talents and skills you use to help them reach their goals. Your employer does not have your well-being anywhere in their long-term goals, nor are they aligned with their bottom line. It is your responsibility to make your contribution in your workspace, and then shut it down when the workday is done.

In the eloquent words of author and speaker Mel Robbins, "no one is coming" to tap you on the shoulder and give you permission to disengage and rest. On the same token, no one is watching you to notice the long hours and unpaid extra tasks you perform on a regular basis. That is not their responsibility. The only person who is responsible for keeping score of your wins is you, my dear. They are not watching, but you can keep track. When it comes time to prove how you made an impact to help the organization reach its goals, you will be ready.

So what does matter to your employer? Remember, they are not watching you because they are watching their own goals. You are one part of a larger system that exists to help them reach those goals. You know how companies pay consultants huge amounts of money to help define and refine their mission and vision statements? They don't do that because it looks good on the front page of the company website. Have you paid attention to annual and quarterly earnings reports? If you admit to not paying attention in the past, consider this your second chance to jump back in and take notice.

The reason for this is for you to understand your employer's big picture. What goals are they aiming to achieve? What metrics are they measuring on a short-term basis in order to reach those annual goals? On a micro level, what metrics are you measured against in your annual performance review? All these elements help you understand the bigger picture and connect the dots for what you can use to prove your impact. Anything else that does not contribute to your company's overall performance means nothing to its bottom line.

So remember this when you think spending long hours planning the office holiday party, or being the one who circulates the birthday card for your boss, means anything to the bottom line. Don't get me wrong. Gestures like that are indeed kind and considerate, but they don't protect professionally. Being a thoughtful team member is a sign that you are a good human being. But your supervisor won't be measuring how great you were at participating in the Secret Santa activities when they score you for your annual performance review. Do those things because they are fun or bring you joy, but not because you think it will earn you any favor at annual review time.

What do you need to track as your receipts? I'm so glad you asked. I've had several opportunities to speak to educators who were looking for a change. Between conference presentations and smaller group gatherings, I have been able to reach quite a few folks in a variety of settings. They showed up to hear advice on preparing for career shifts, and each had several things in common. They had long careers in education, probably as top performers. Their reasons for wanting a career change varied from suffering burnout to pursuing leadership roles. The look in their eyes was all the same...hopeful and fearful. They desperately wanted a roadmap, a path to get from where they are to where they want to be. They want that path to be safe and comfortable, along with some guarantee that they will be rewarded at their new destination.

At each gathering, I opened with one question. I asked them to explain why they deserve the next thing they are seeking. Each time, I was met with blank stares. I offered vague clarifiers, but still pushed them to explain why anyone should believe they were worthy of that new position or promotion. Some felt indignant at my blunt opener, and some looked defeated because they had no answer. My challenge was simple. The next time someone poses that question to them, they need to be ready with a solid response. "Start collecting your own receipts" was my charge. No one is keeping score of your good performance at your job. No one will knock on your door to deliver opportunities to you. That is all your responsibility. You are the only one who can craft your entire narrative about your impact and contributions.

Let me back this up with more than just advice. There is research behind this. Professionals who actively track their accomplishments are significantly more likely to experience career growth. A 2025 feature from *Journaling Insights*, drawing on recent McKinsey data, found that individuals who maintained a consistent record of their achievements through a personal career journal were 42 percent more likely to earn a promotion within two years. That is not a small bump. It is evidence that reflection paired with documentation can shift your entire trajectory. This confirms what I have been telling my coaching clients for years: your brilliance cannot just live in your head. It has to live on paper or in the cloud.

Remember my failed first attempt to negotiate a raise in my education role? Yeah, don't be like me. I made some big, incorrect assumptions that the decision makers would somehow understand my impact on the organization just from memory. That humiliating lesson lives in my head on repeat and fuels my intention of teaching as many midlifers as possible to not fall into the trap of false professional security. You will have to create your own scorecard and keep it updated. Get it out of your head that tracking your wins is being braggadocious. At the bare minimum, it is for survival. At best, it will be your leverage for better pay when you are in any professional negotiations.

The academic space supports this message. A 2024 article in *PRiMER* by Campbell and Rodríguez emphasized that faculty members who carefully structured their CVs by tracking awards, initiatives, and leadership contributions over time were more successful in securing tenure and promotion. Most of us at this age are not chasing tenure, but the lesson still applies. When your impact is clearly documented, it becomes visible and persuasive to decision-makers.

Other fields reflect the same principle. Researchers Migliore and Butterworth (2021) found that documenting success metrics in vocational and employment settings led to improved job outcomes. This finding applies to anyone in the workforce, regardless of age. Share this with your young adult children who are stepping into the workforce for the first time, too. Tracking the right kind of information, such as how your project increased efficiency, saved money, or improved satisfaction, gives you leverage when it is time to negotiate, advocate, or transition.

The importance of self-awareness and tracking success starts early. A 2022 study in *Frontiers in Education* examined how students' awareness of their skills and accomplishments shaped their confidence and readiness to pursue opportunities. While the study focused on students, the insight applies to professionals at every stage. Clarity about what you have done strengthens confidence in what comes next. That kind of confidence is powerful.

Organizations are already investing in systems that track accomplishments with intention. The BUILD program, for example, uses annual snapshots to monitor alumni outcomes and store contributions for future reference (Zúñiga & Colbern, 2022). You can take a page from that approach by creating your own quarterly snapshot. Keep a running list of your wins, your contributions, and the results. It does not have to be elaborate. It just needs to be consistent and easy to access when the right opportunity presents itself.

No one needs to hand you a formal award for your contributions to matter. You can acknowledge yourself by collecting, organizing, and naming your impact. These receipts are not just sentimental records. They are professional currency. Job titles may come and go.

Your documented value stays with you. It is yours to own, showcase, and use as leverage for the career you deserve.

Shifting that mindset for educators is tough. There is a spirit of altruism in K12 education that encourages us to always put the kids first. I don't argue against putting kids first, because that is indeed the whole point of the work. However, that message has been abused over time, where educators put the kids first and then forget to put themselves on the list at all. They give and give and give, but leave no space to refill their own empty cups. They sacrifice willingly, but are left feeling overlooked when recognition doesn't come their way. When these dedicated educators decide they are ready to level up into something more, it comes after a long period of doing all the right things, but not keeping records of those accomplishments. When it is time to advocate for their worthiness during a career shift, it is a sad scramble to collect artifacts that tell the right story of who they are and what they can do.

If this is your situation, here is my rough, unapologetic advice. Start collecting everything that celebrates you professionally and save it in a digital space. If you receive performance accolades from your supervisor via email, flag it and save it in a folder. If you were part of a collaborative team that delivered a superior project, outline your contribution and what was accomplished. If you earned a new certification, post it on your LinkedIn profile.

Follow my steps below to get you started in the right direction.

1. **Create a folder** in your personal private cloud account (Google Drive, OneDrive, etc.) and start adding these items to it any chance you get. Keep it organized so you can find items and pull from it quickly when an opportunity arises.

2. **Collect visuals of the experiences**. If you delivered a presentation, have someone snap a few photos of you in the act. If you led or participated in a collaborative group, take screenshots or pics of the deliverables.

3. **Know your numbers.** The soft story of each event matters, but being able to measure the impact is critical. Did your contribution result in a positive increase in revenue? Was there a percentage boost in student achievement? Did you save the organization money by staying under budget or finding new funding opportunities?

Remember my original question: why do you deserve the job opportunity you seek? If you begin collecting these professional artifacts, it will become easier to draft a narrative to adequately respond to the question. You will look back at these items and feel positively empowered to represent yourself on the journey to your next phase. Don't delay. Your story started a long time ago. Don't let any more days pass without documenting the experience.

### Maya's Wake-Up Call

Maya had always believed that hard work spoke for itself. She wasn't flashy. She didn't brag. She didn't need the spotlight. What she needed was to feel proud of the work she did, and she was. Maya showed up early, stayed late, volunteered for the stretch projects, the fire drills, and the after-hours team events. She was the quiet rock of her department. She was dependable, graceful, and consistent. Her performance reviews were always solid, her colleagues leaned on her, and her leaders trusted her to get things done.

She thought that would be enough. So when Maya's name didn't make the short list for a long-anticipated leadership role, the one she had practically built from scratch, she was stunned. Then she was embarrassed. Later, she quietly grew resentful.

In her mind, there was no way her company couldn't see how instrumental she'd been. She had given her all to that place. So why wasn't that loyalty being returned?

The answer came during a difficult conversation with her mentor. Maya had gone to her, venting and trying to make sense of what had happened. After a long pause, her mentor gently asked, "What did you submit with your application?"

"Just my résumé and cover letter," Maya replied. "You know my work speaks for itself."

Her mentor shook her head slowly. "Maya, you've been doing great work for twenty years. But they don't remember the presentation you saved in 2017. Or the policy you rewrote in 2019. Or how you coached the entire new hire cohort in 2020. None of that is in your file unless you put it there. You didn't collect your receipts."

That moment hit Maya like a punch to the gut. She realized that while she had been focused on doing the work, she had neglected to document it, speak on it, and strategically highlight it. Her brilliance had become background noise. It was familiar, reliable, but invisible.

It wasn't malicious. It wasn't even personal. It was just the nature of the workplace. People remember what you remind them of. Maya had been silently excellent for so long that her achievements had faded into the scenery. Meanwhile, others who had kept a running list, updated their profiles, shared wins in meetings, or sent quarterly highlight emails were moving ahead.

Maya's first emotion was bitterness. She felt let down, not just by her company, but by the unwritten rules that no one had ever explained to her. Eventually, the bitterness gave way to something more productive: clarity.

She started keeping a digital brag folder. Every time she led a project, received a glowing email, solved a tough problem, or mentored a colleague, she dropped it in the folder. She updated her LinkedIn profile and added real results. She requested feedback in writing. She practiced talking about her wins with confidence, not arrogance.

She started collecting her receipts because she finally understood that excellence without evidence can cost you opportunities.

Now, Maya teaches every woman in her network to do the same. She tells them, "If you don't write your story, someone else will, and they won't always get it right."

So let me ask you this. Have you been so focused on the *doing* that you've forgotten the *documenting*? Can you easily list five things you accomplished at work this year? Do you have a system to track your impact, your growth, your wins?

If not, it's time to start. You don't need to wait for a formal review or a promotion opportunity. You don't need to be in the middle of a job search. You need to start now, right where you are. Your story deserves to be told, and no one can tell it better than you.

Collect your receipts. Then the next time an opportunity knocks, you'll have the portfolio, the presence, and the proof to walk through that door like you belong there. That's because you do.

## Why You Need to Track Your Brilliance

In my conversation with Trisha Simone Vincent, personal branding expert and founder of *Launch Your Influence*, she reminded us that our resumes and reputations are often shaped by what we choose to document. It's not necessarily shaped by what we did, but by what we're able to prove.

Her story echoed mine. After years of corporate and executive leadership, we both realized we had no tangible record of our brilliance. There was no database of impact. We both just had a growing sense of burnout and an identity crisis creeping in when we imagined life beyond our current titles.

What saved us? Receipts. Trisha said it best: "Your title is rented, but your character, your contribution, your value, that's yours to own."

Be really honest with yourself. Nobody is going to collect this data for you.

## The Silence is Costing You

When you don't track your wins, you limit your power to negotiate, pivot, and present yourself with confidence. I've worked with brilliant Black women in their 50s who couldn't recall their last big project or quantify their leadership impact because the receipts weren't in hand. They were hidden in old emails, buried in memory, or locked in someone else's HR system.

That kind of silence keeps you underpaid, under-acknowledged, and undervalued. Silence won't get you seen. Only you can change that.

## Build Your Receipt Collection System

Here's how to take your value out of your brain and into a system:

### 1. Start with Performance Reviews

If you're still employed, revisit your past 3–5 years of evaluations. These are full of data points you've probably forgotten: budget impacts, process improvements, team growth, client outcomes. Highlight every metric, milestone, and comment that reflects your contribution.

### 2. Reverse Engineer Your Impact

Can't remember specifics? Ask yourself: *If I didn't do this work, what would have gone wrong?* That's your value. That's the hidden impact you've been downplaying.

### 3. Phone a Friend

Reach out to trusted colleagues from different chapters of your career and ask: *What did you always count on me for?* You'll hear things that surprise you. There are gifts you didn't know you had, strengths you forgot to claim.

## 4. Keep a Running Log

Set up a simple Google Doc or Notes app folder called "Career Receipts." Every time you finish a project, solve a problem, or get praise, write it down. You'll thank yourself later.

## 5. Own Your Outcomes

Facts win negotiations. You can't make bold career moves without evidence. When you walk into that interview, pitch your next client, or ask for a raise. You won't guess. You'll *present*.

## Your Legacy Deserves Proof

You are not just updating a resume or chasing a promotion. You are documenting a legacy. Every performance review, every project win, every moment you led with clarity and excellence adds to that legacy. If you follow the steps I laid out. Revisit your past reviews, reverse engineer your impact, talk to people who have witnessed your brilliance, keep a running log, and own your outcomes. You will begin to build something far more powerful than just a brag sheet. You will create a living, breathing archive of your professional story. Plus, it will be a story that you control.

Your receipts are not just for job interviews or performance evaluations. They are for every room you plan to walk into with confidence. They are for the proposal you want to submit, the keynote you want to pitch, the business you are ready to launch, or the consulting path you are finally exploring. This is not busy work. This is visibility work.

Your story deserves to be told with evidence. Your brilliance deserves to be remembered, recognized, and rewarded. Your value should not be buried in forgotten email threads, outdated job descriptions, or the silent corners of your own memory. Pull it out. Give it shape. Give it language.

Every person I've worked with who felt stuck or overlooked eventually realized the same truth. It was never about starting over. It was about starting to collect. When they began tracking their contributions with intention, the clarity came. The confidence came. The opportunities followed.

This work is ongoing, but it is not hard. You are already doing the things. Now, make them visible. Make them count.

So let me say it one more time for the people in the back: Collect your receipts. Document the details. Organize your greatness. Present your impact. You have already done the work. Now build the system that proves it, because silence won't get you seen. Guessing won't get you paid. Receipts will. Use the activity below to help get started with your own receipts system.

## Part 1: Inventory Your Impact

Reflect on three meaningful projects, initiatives, or roles you've led or contributed to in the past five years.

1.  What problem did this work solve?

2.  What was the outcome or measurable result?

3.  Who specifically benefited or was positively impacted?

4.  What role did you play in making it successful?

Now revisit your last two performance reviews (or any past feedback you can access):

- What positive feedback stood out to you?

- Are there any numbers, outcomes, or wins that deserve to be highlighted?

- What soft skills or leadership qualities do people often associate with you?

**Part 2: Reverse Engineer Your Value**

Choose one position or project and complete this sentence:

*If I hadn't _____, then _____ wouldn't have happened.*

Now turn that insight into a concise bullet point that could be used on your resume, LinkedIn profile, or elevator pitch. Keep it focused on outcomes and your unique role.

Example:

*Led redesign of staff onboarding process, reducing training time by 35% and improving first-year retention.*

**Part 3: Create Your Receipt Tracker**

Use the simple format below to begin documenting your career wins in a centralized folder (Google Drive, OneDrive, or wherever is easiest for you to access).

| Date | Project / Task | Your Contribution | Outcome or Result | Evidence (email, report, etc.) |
|------|------|------|------|------|
| 03/2022 | Virtual parent workshop | Designed & facilitated session | 94% satisfaction rating | Survey feedback PDF |
| 07/2023 | LMS migration initiative | Trained staff, managed vendors | On time, under budget | Project brief & budget sheet |

**Journal Prompts**

These reflection questions are designed to spark clarity and shift your mindset from modesty to ownership:

- What have I told myself about not being "accomplished enough" to track my wins?

- What's one career moment I'm quietly proud of but haven't shared with anyone?

- How would it feel to walk into a meeting, negotiation, or interview with full confidence in my value?

- What is one small step I can take this week to begin collecting my career receipts?

# CHAPTER 5

## They Forgot What You Did. Don't You Dare: How to brand, pitch, and promote yourself with receipts, not regret

If you've ever been told, "You're doing such a great job, we'd be lost without you," only to be skipped over when it was time for promotions or recognition, you're not alone. Midlife professionals, especially Black women, are often the backbones of teams, the fixers, the dependable ones. But here's the catch: being dependable isn't a job title. Loyalty, as powerful as it sounds, doesn't guarantee you'll be remembered when it counts.

That's why you've got to remember for them.

You are the archivist of your own excellence. The storyteller of your own impact. It's not enough to have done the work. You have to package it, pitch it, and promote it. You're not doing this from a place of ego, but from a place of clarity. You see, the promotion, the new opportunity, or the partnership. They don't go to the silent contributors. They go to the ones who show their work. We are taking the lessons you just learned about the value of collecting your receipts and putting them into action. Your next objective is to build your personal brand.

A personal brand is simply the story people tell about you when you're not in the room, and the story you choose to help them tell. It's not about logos, followers, or being an influencer. It's about clarity and consistency. Your personal brand is built from how you show up, what you're known for, and how you articulate your value in a way that aligns with your goals. For midlife professionals, especially those of us who have spent decades letting our work speak for itself, this concept might feel unfamiliar or even uncomfortable at first. But here's the truth: people remember what you repeat, not just what you've done. Your personal brand is your opportunity to shape the narrative, to ensure that your strengths, values, and vision are not just visible but unforgettable. It's how you move from being the best-kept secret to being top of mind when opportunities arise.

**Let's Break It Down:**

**1. Branding Begins With Clarity**

If you can't articulate who you are and what you do in two sentences, you're not ready. Midlife branding isn't about a logo or fancy colors. It's about communicating your *value proposition*. What are you known for? What do people count on you to deliver? If your name comes up in a meeting, what do you want it attached to?

Write your own headline. "I help districts implement digital tools that improve student outcomes." Or "I lead operational teams through messy transitions with clarity and calm." If your name was a LinkedIn banner, what would it say?

**2. Pitch With Proof, Not Personality**

It's tempting to believe that "being nice," "being reliable," or "being a team player" will get you noticed, but that's just not reality. Organizations reward results, not personality. That means your pitch has to include *receipts*. Remember, these have to be quantifiable, concrete, and contextual wins. If your last initiative improved customer engagement by 22%, say that. If you trained 45 people and launched a system in 30 days, put it in writing. Numbers give your story teeth.

## 3. Promote Strategically (and Regularly)

This is not about bragging. This is about visibility. Start where you're comfortable. This might look like posting on LinkedIn, publishing internal newsletters, and department meetings. Share updates. Speak on panels. Volunteer to present results. You can be humble *and* visible. The key is consistency. Treat your career like a brand campaign. You will need to keep your wins circulating.

## 4. Know the Difference Between Praise and Power

Praise is someone clapping for you. Power is having the leverage to make moves. If you've been praised but not promoted, it's time to shift the strategy. Go from being seen as "helpful" to being known as "high impact." By keeping track of your receipts, you can turn those compliments into currency.

## 5. From Invisible to Irreplaceable

Stop waiting for someone to notice your effort. That's a trap. Instead, use your receipts to frame your own narrative. Build a portfolio. Update your LinkedIn. Rewrite your resume bullets. When you walk into that next opportunity, whether it's an interview, an evaluation, or a reinvention, you'll already have the evidence to back up your brilliance.

## Now That You're Seen, Let's Make Sure You're Heard: Time to Update That Resume

So here you are. Your profile is set up, the new headshot is uploaded, and you have a headline that is tightened. You've started to peek out from behind the curtain on LinkedIn. Maybe you've even liked a post or sent a few connection requests. That's big.

But now you're starting to wonder: *If someone actually reaches out… is my resume even ready?*

Or worse: *When's the last time I even looked at it?*

Cue the full-body cringe.

For many midlife professionals, the resume is where the panic sets in. It feels like trying to resurrect a version of yourself that doesn't quite fit anymore. Your last job search might've involved printing out paper copies of your resume at Staples and dropping them off in person. This is back when face-to-face impressions could save a mediocre document.

Now? Your resume has to work harder. It has to stand on its own in an online system before a human ever sees it. It needs to speak clearly, confidently, and concisely. So yes, it needs to evolve just like you have.

Let's walk through how to do that without losing your mind.

### It's Not Just a List. It's a Highlight Reel

If your current resume reads like a job description, we need to change that today. Listing your responsibilities might sound logical, but it doesn't tell your story. It doesn't showcase your impact.

Here's the shift:

- Instead of: "Responsible for managing budgets."
- Try: "Managed a $2.5M annual budget across three departments, reallocating funds to reduce waste and support new digital initiatives."

That second version shows action, scale, and results. It paints a picture.

That's what hiring managers want to see, not just what you were *assigned*. It's about what you *accomplished*.

### Don't Let Humility Be Your Handicap

Let's address something head-on: midlife women of color are often socialized not to brag. We downplay our wins, we shrug off our brilliance, and we quietly carry entire teams on our backs without ever updating the bullet points on our resumes. Stop it.

This is your permission slip: Your resume is not the place to be humble.

It's your billboard. It should say, loudly and clearly, "Here's what I've done. Here's what I can do again. Here's the kind of magic I bring to a team."

You're not embellishing. You're telling the truth, unapologetically. You've earned that.

## Start with a Powerful Summary

The top third of your resume is prime real estate. That summary section should feel like your personal mission statement. Many recruiters and hiring managers admit that the top third of your resume is all they actually read in most cases.

It should answer:

- How many years of experience do you have?
- What industries or sectors have you worked in?
- What are your top skills or contributions?
- What results have you delivered?

Here's a formula to try:

"20+ years in K-12 and higher education, leading districtwide innovation and professional learning initiatives. Developed programs that increased teacher satisfaction by 50% and improved student outcomes across three school districts. Currently seeking opportunities to bring strategic digital transformation to mission-driven organizations."

That's you. That's your value. There is no fluff and no filler. It contains just facts and focus.

**Only Show What Moves the Needle**

I know it's hard, but resist the urge to include every job you've ever had. What you did in 1998 might have been groundbreaking, but if it's not relevant to the direction you're headed now, it doesn't belong.

Stick to the most recent 10–12 years of experience, unless an older role directly supports your current pivot.

For each role, keep it tight:

- Include a 1–2 sentence description of the company or team.

- Follow with 5–7 powerful bullet points that focus on achievements, not tasks.

- Quantify results when possible. (Increased enrollment by 25%. Reduced errors by 40%. Cut onboarding time in half.)

Every bullet should answer the question: *Why did this matter?*

**Two Pages Max. Seriously.**

I know you've done a lot. I know you've had a career full of incredible moments.

But recruiters don't have the time, or the patience, to read a 4-page resume.

The best resumes are brief, strategic, and tailored. They don't tell your whole life story. They tell the *right* story for the opportunity you want next.

If it doesn't serve that story, let it go.

**Bonus Tip: Write the Cover Letter**

Yes, it still matters. Even in the age of job portals and digital uploads.

Your cover letter is your chance to speak directly to the hiring manager. It allows you to connect the dots, explain your pivot, and make your case in a warm, narrative way, just like we've done here. The truth is, most people skip it. Which means *you* stand out just for sending one.

**From Basic to Bold: Transforming a Resume Bullet That Tells Your Story**

Let's start with a common example:

**Before:**

"Responsible for coordinating teacher professional development sessions."

This is technically true, but it doesn't *show* anything. There's no scope, no result, no ownership. It sounds like a task someone was assigned, not a leadership move someone owned.

Let's transform it by asking a few key questions:

1. **What was the *scale* of this work?**

   How many sessions? How many educators? Districtwide or school-based?

2. **What was the *impact* of these sessions?**

   Did it lead to increased engagement, improved outcomes, and stronger retention?

3. **What *skills* were demonstrated?**

   Strategic planning, curriculum design, public speaking, tech integration?

**After:**

"Designed and led over 25 districtwide professional development sessions for 300+ educators, resulting in a 40% increase in implementation of digital learning strategies across K–12 classrooms."

Now we've got:

- Action ("Designed and led")
- Scale ("25 districtwide sessions" and "300+ educators")
- Results ("40% increase in implementation")
- Context (focused on digital learning, relevant to modern hiring needs)

Let's try another one:

**Before:**

"Managed school budgets and supplies."

Basic. Boring. Easily ignored.

**After:**

"Oversaw a $1.2M school budget and streamlined purchasing processes, reducing supply costs by 15% while meeting all compliance and instructional needs."

We've added:

- Ownership and leadership
- A quantifiable financial result
- Evidence of strategic thinking

One more for those transitioning careers:

**Before:**

"Taught 9th-grade history."

Straightforward—but this doesn't help someone pivoting into instructional design, program management, or edtech.

**After:**

"Developed and delivered an engaging U.S. History curriculum for 120+ students annually, integrating digital platforms and project-based learning to boost student performance and digital literacy."

That shows:

- Curriculum design
- Tech integration
- Classroom management at scale
- Student-centered outcomes

## LinkedIn Is Your Newest Power Tool, Even If You're Just Getting Started

When I first logged into LinkedIn with fresh eyes and a fresh purpose, I wasn't trying to go viral or rack up a hundred job offers overnight. I was simply trying to be seen.

After two decades of building a career, leading teams, earning accolades, and showing up early and staying late, I wasn't seen. Somehow, I still felt invisible in the digital space. My resume told one story. But what about my online presence? It was barely whispering.

That's when it hit me. If I wanted to be found for the kind of work I truly wanted to do next, I had to stop being shy about showing up.

### Facing the Fear of Being Seen

Let's name the thing out loud: building your personal brand online can feel deeply uncomfortable. It's not just about picking a profile picture or crafting a catchy headline. It's about declaring, publicly, that you believe in your own value. That you're ready to be visible. For many of us, especially women of color in midlife, that goes against everything we were taught.

We were trained to be the behind-the-scenes glue. We were the steady hand, or the fixer. We were comfortable being the get-it-done-without-fanfare one. We weren't always taught how to promote ourselves. We were taught to keep our heads down, be grateful, and not make too much noise.

So now, when LinkedIn asks you to upload a photo, write a summary, and speak confidently about your experience, your first instinct might be to shrink. Worse, you tend to stall and second-guess. Maybe you've even said things like:

- "I don't want to sound like I'm bragging."
- "What if no one cares what I have to say?"
- "I'm not even sure what my brand is."

If that's you, I see you. I've been you. You're not wrong for feeling that way. But I promise, you're not alone. It is possible to take one small step at a time and still be moving forward.

## Why It Matters (Especially Now)

Here's the truth: in today's professional world, you don't just need to be good at what you do. You need to be *visible* doing it.

You may have the degrees, the certifications, the experience, and the receipts to prove your impact. But unless people can find you, learn about you, and understand how you think, the result is simple. You'll be overlooked. It isn't because you're not brilliant, but because you're invisible in the spaces where decisions are being made.

I know that sounds harsh. I wish it weren't true. But the job market, speaking engagements, consulting contracts, and leadership invitations? They go to the people who are findable and top-of-mind. LinkedIn is the most powerful platform for making that happen.

If you've started breaking out in a cold sweat, stay with me. This isn't about becoming an overnight influencer. It's about owning your voice. It's about telling your story your way before someone else tells it for you, or forgets to tell it at all.

It's about being intentional, even if you're introverted. It's about choosing not to disappear into the background at a time in life when your wisdom, your experience, and your perspective have never been more needed.

## A New Way to Be Seen

Think of your LinkedIn profile as the cover of your next chapter. It's not your whole life story. It's a curated window that gives people a glimpse of what you've done and where you're headed. Start simple.

Upload a headshot that feels true to who you are now. We are not pushing the corporate version of you from 15 years ago. We want the one who has lived, learned, and grown into this moment. Then write a headline that reflects the value you bring. Don't just put your job title. Put your impact.

"Instructional Designer | Creating learning experiences that empower educators and transform classrooms."

That's clarity. That's confidence. It starts to build your personal brand.

Your summary? Just use a few sentences. It needs to be in your voice and include your why. Articulate what lights you up. Speak on what you've done. Lay out where you're headed. That's it.

Then, just breathe. Let that be enough for now.

## Reimagining "Networking"

I know what you might be thinking. This still feels like too much. That's fair. So let's reframe this idea of networking.

Forget the awkward small talk, the cheesy introductions, the feeling like you're bothering someone. Networking on LinkedIn isn't

MELANATED MIDLIFE      91

about begging for attention. It's about building a community of aligned people who see you, value you, and might even open doors you didn't know existed.

Every comment you leave, every thoughtful post you share, every person you reconnect with, are tiny ripples. Those ripples grow. Start with people you already know. Then follow companies that inspire you. Join groups that speak to your interests. Let your curiosity lead you, not your fear. You don't need to be perfect. You just need to be present.

**Taking the First Steps: You Don't Have to Do It All Today**

If you're still with me, you've already done something powerful. You've opened your heart and mind to the idea that maybe, just maybe, there's something on the other side of this discomfort. Maybe you are beginning to understand that building your personal brand online isn't vanity. It's a strategy. It's survival. It's self-respect.

Now let's talk about how to actually begin. You don't need to do everything in one sitting. This isn't a sprint. It's a slow, steady reclaiming of your space in the professional world. It starts with the basics.

**Step 1: Set Up or Revisit Your Profile**

If you haven't created a LinkedIn profile yet, now's the time. If you have one but haven't touched it since 2012, that's okay too. Start fresh, with no shame.

Start with the easy wins:

- **Upload a recent photo.** One where you feel like you. It doesn't have to be a formal headshot. Just make sure it's clear, well-lit, and shows the confidence you've earned.

- **Choose a banner image.** LinkedIn gives you a default one, but this is an opportunity to make your page more personal. You can upload a simple photo of a city skyline, your workspace, or something that subtly reflects your field or personality.

- **Update your headline.** This is the little line that appears under your name. Instead of just saying "Administrative Assistant" or "Educator," try something like:

"Experienced Project Manager | Helping Teams Deliver Results with Calm and Clarity" or "Career Coach for Midlife Professionals | Empowering Reinvention with Purpose & Strategy"

The headline is searchable, so think of it as your digital handshake. Short, sharp, and full of promise.

## Step 2: Write Your "About" Summary

This one might take some time, and that's okay.

Think of this as the conversation you'd have with someone over coffee who asked, "So what do you do, and what are you looking to do next?"

Your summary should answer three simple questions:

- Who are you?
- What are you great at?
- What are you passionate about or working toward?

Here's a little template to get your wheels turning:

"I'm a [Profession] with over [X years] of experience in [Industry or Specialty]. I specialize in [Key Skills or Impact Areas] and am passionate about [Passion or Purpose]. My career has been driven by [Brief Philosophy or Approach], and I'm currently exploring new opportunities to [Goal or Outcome]."

This is your value statement, and it serves multiple purposes. Don't worry about sounding polished. Aim for clarity and heart. Speak like you're talking to someone who genuinely wants to help you succeed.

## Step 3: Add Your Experience (Without Overthinking)

This isn't a copy-paste of your entire resume. You're just giving people context. Think of each job entry as a little chapter in your career journey.

For each role:

- List the job title and company.
- Add 2–3 bullet points that highlight your impact.
- Use active verbs: led, organized, increased, supported, and built.
- If possible, add numbers or results, but only if they make sense.

This is your time to stop being modest. Tell the truth about the value you've brought.

## Step 4: Start Making Meaningful Connections

Now that your profile is starting to reflect who you really are, it's time to invite people into your virtual world.

Start with low-hanging fruit:

- Former coworkers
- Friends in your industry
- People you've met at past trainings, events, or conferences
- Mentors or mentees

When you send a connection request, add a personal note. Here's a script that feels warm but professional:

"Hi Jasmine, I loved working with you at ABC Schools! I'm reconnecting with colleagues as I grow my network here on LinkedIn. I would love to stay in touch."

It's not about numbers. It's about relationships. Relationships start with realness.

## Step 5: Engage (Quietly, if You Need To)

You don't have to post right away. Just start by watching, liking, and reading. Leave a thoughtful comment on something that resonates with you. Share an article with a few lines about why it mattered to you.

These small steps are how you begin building visibility, not with a megaphone, but with presence. Over time, that presence becomes power.

# CHAPTER 6

## It's Not Too Late to Start Over. Again: I Was Not Ready When I Experienced a Job Loss

I've coached people through job loss and transitions. I've led workshops on how to bounce back from career setbacks. I've spoken on panels, given keynotes, and created downloadable guides for folks in midlife facing career transitions. So, you would think that when it happened to me, I'd be ready. But let me be honest with you. I was not.

My layoff from my corporate job came unexpectedly. The job required a lot of business travel, so on that day, I was confidently presenting like I had done countless times before. That morning, a company-wide email had been sent from the CEO. She shared in an expectedly somber tone that there would be a reduction in force. Some coworkers would be receiving notices later in the day to meet with HR. We all knew there was nothing anyone could do except wait to find out if they were affected. The scramble of texting my work buddies began to find out who, if any of us, had received a notice yet. Everyone appeared to be in the clear, so I continued on with my day.

Keep in mind, I was on a business trip that day. I had customers to connect with and a presentation to deliver in front of a large group of university tech directors. While I was reviewing my notes, I received an email notification from an unfamiliar name, telling me (not asking) to be present on a virtual call that would be happening in an hour. Although in disbelief, I instantly knew what that was. I was losing my job. A short while later, I was on a call with an HR representative, hearing carefully scripted, polite words that did nothing to soften the blow. Was this really happening, or had there been a mistake? Were they really laying me off while I was actively on a business trip for them, two states away from home?

At first, I wasn't scared. Truly, I wasn't. I thought, "Okay, I've got the tools. I've got the network. I know what to do." I gave myself a three-month runway to find my next job role. Maybe it could take four months tops. I told myself I'd land something quickly because I had the experience and the receipts. Honey, was I wrong! It took seven. Seven long, soul-testing months is how long it took me to find my next job.

## The Silence Will Shake You

During that time, I experienced the kind of quiet that makes you question everything. I went from being an expert to feeling invisible. My inbox either stayed empty or was bombarded with a rush of automated rejection emails from non-human AI systems. Recruiters stopped calling. Applications went into black holes. I started wondering if I had imagined my past success, if maybe I wasn't as valuable as I thought.

That's the thing nobody tells you about job loss. It's not just the income that disappears. It's also your identity. Your confidence and daily routine are all tied to that job, frankly, because you spend the most time there. It's the version of yourself that you've grown comfortable with. Think of any time we introduce ourselves in new circles. Right after knowing your name, they ask, "What do you do?". Your response to that simple question tells the other person everything they care to know about you right up front. It roughly reveals your income bracket, your skill set, and maybe what professional circles you have access to. When that goes, you're left standing in front of a mirror, asking: Who am I without the title?

I allowed myself two whole days to sit in my hole of self-pity. The shock of being laid off was fresh. My ego was more bruised than anything. They laid me off? I'm special. They like me. People were happy to have me on the team, right? News of my layoff would send shockwaves throughout the organization, wouldn't it? People would march out of the building in protest of such an unjust thing happening to someone they universally loved. Hadn't I built relationships with the right people to insulate me from this kind of thing? In those quiet, closed-door conversations about who on the team was expendable, wouldn't my name be on the short list of folks they couldn't work without? Obviously, that wasn't the case. I wasn't special when it came down to headcount or budget. It was a business, and my employment was no longer needed in this organization. I had to pick up my damaged ego and piece together my dignity without looking too hurt. But I was hurt. I was embarrassed. I felt like I had been kicked off the cool kids team for having cooties or something.

These feelings had to be suppressed quickly. There just wasn't time to wallow in this space too long. By the third day, I began putting my own job search strategies into play. The first step was to reach out to my professional community and share that I was no longer with the company due to a reduction in force. The focus was to keep my tone professional without showing any emotion about my circumstances. Being outwardly emotional might create cracks in my armor, and I didn't want that. My goal was to appear in control and ready for the next phase of whatever was happening. I had to at least act like I knew what I was doing, even if I was scared shitless. I chose to message people individually through private messages on professional social media platforms. Putting that "open to work" banner on my LinkedIn profile was just too pitiful in my opinion. That was for desperate people, and I was determined to look like I was in control. Looking like I knew how to navigate this chess game was critical.

I'll admit, writing this is a little uncomfortable.

Not because I'm afraid to share, but because I thought I had it all figured out. I'm someone who *teaches* others how to navigate career transitions. I've coached midlife professionals through layoffs, helped them rewrite their résumés, rebuild their confidence, and land new opportunities. I've given presentations on this very topic.

What I thought would be a professional reset turned into a deeply personal journey. I faced self-doubt, financial pressure, identity questions, and plenty of silence in between the rare interview invites. I learned that *knowing what to do* and actually *living through it* are two very different things.

That's why I'm sharing this. It's not because I have the perfect formula, but because I've been in it. If you're in it too, or ever find yourself navigating uncertainty or transition, maybe something in my story will help you feel less alone and a little more equipped.

## The Truth About the Job Market

## The Timeline Is Not Yours to Control

A tough, humbling lesson I learned during this job search was how easy it is to underestimate the time it takes to land your next role, even when you're doing everything right.

Going into this, I genuinely thought three to four months would be enough. I was diligent, focused, and didn't waste time. I took three days after my layoff to regroup, and then I got straight to work, without a sabbatical and no extended break to "find myself." Jumping straight into the grind was my tactic, going through job boards, applications, interviews, networking, and follow-ups. Yet still, it took seven months.

Some of that, of course, wasn't about me. In 2025, we are in a very strange season, both economically and politically. The job market is tighter, slower, and more complex than it's been in a long time. I had a candid conversation with a close friend who is a former senior vice president at a major recruiting firm. She told me plainly: "This is the worst I've ever seen the market in all my decades in the industry." That conversation was a turning point for me. Not because it solved anything, but because it reminded me that this wasn't all on me. I wasn't broken. My résumé wasn't trash. My effort wasn't off track. The market itself was struggling, and no amount of productivity can outwork a stalled economy.

What I *did* have was a cushion. Believe me, I acknowledge that with full humility and gratitude. I had a severance package. It was a modest one, but helpful. I filed for unemployment immediately and didn't hesitate to make use of what I was eligible for. I also had savings. Those resources didn't last forever, but they carried me through in phases: first the severance money, then the unemployment payouts, and finally, dipping into our savings for the final stretch.

If there's advice I'd give to someone preparing for a career transition or facing a layoff, it's this: prepare for a longer timeline than you think, even if you're highly qualified. Be prepared if you're doing everything "right." Be financially and mentally ready for the long haul. This is especially important if, like me, you plan to hit the ground running and don't want, or can't afford, an extended pause.

What I know now is this: the job search isn't just a professional process; it's an emotional and financial endurance test. The better prepared you are to weather it, the more clarity and confidence you can maintain while you wait for the right door to open.

I want to say this loud and clear for anyone going through it right now: The job market doesn't move on your personal timeline. I hit the ground running. I didn't take a break, didn't go "find myself," didn't even pause to decompress. I updated my resume, brushed up on my portfolio, and started applying to roles immediately. Yet still, months passed.

So if you're out there wondering why your inbox is quiet, please know it's not always about you.

## Your Network Is Your Lifeline

If there's one lesson I want you to tattoo on your midlife heart, it's this: Your next opportunity will not come from a cold job board. It will come from people. Prioritize relationships over resumes.

One of the most eye-opening lessons I learned during my seven-month job search was the real power of reaching out to my professional network. I say that as someone who teaches this principle to others. Still, living it firsthand gave me a deeper appreciation for just how critical personal connections truly are.

Even with all my experience and insider knowledge of how hiring works, I spent several hours each day applying for jobs online. I can't even tell you how many applications I submitted. It blurs together after a while. The process itself isn't particularly hard. It's just...empty. Automated. Digital. Impersonal. You upload your résumé, answer some screening questions, and click submit. Most of the time, it feels like shouting into a void. You don't interact with a human being unless a recruiter happens to flag your application and reaches out for one of those standard 15-minute phone screeners.

What I found, however, is that the real traction —the interviews that actually went somewhere —came when a person was involved. It was the referral from a friend who gave me a heads-up about an opening. It was a colleague who passed my name along or made an introduction. Those moments of human connection were the true doors opening, not the digital application portals.

In hindsight, I should have flipped my strategy. Instead of spending the majority of my time on job boards and application portals, I should have invested most of that energy into reaching out.

That means having conversations, reconnecting with former colleagues, letting people know what I was looking for and what I was qualified to do. The truth is, resumes rarely speak as loudly as relationships do.

It was former colleagues, friends of friends, even podcast listeners who passed my name along, made introductions, or dropped me into conversations I didn't even know were happening. Looking back, I should've spent less time hitting "submit" on applications and more time reconnecting, updating people on my journey, and having real conversations.

Your resume gets scanned. Your relationships get remembered.

## Care for Yourself Like It's a Priority, Because It Is

When you're in a long job search, especially after a layoff, it's easy to treat the process like a full-time job. While I absolutely believe in being proactive, I also learned how critical it is to care for your whole self in the middle of it all. That means physically, emotionally, and intellectually.

In those seven months, my daily routine began to take shape. Every morning, I was up, dressed, laptop open, tracking leads, sending follow-ups. But working that hard in solitude wears on your spirit.

There were days when I cried. Days when I felt numb. Days when I looked at the ceiling and whispered, "Is this it?"

I'm so grateful for my husband. He made me laugh when I couldn't find joy. He reminded me that this wasn't the end of my story. It was just a plot twist.

I also had to fight for my own well-being. I walked daily. I drank the water. I ate nourishing food, even when I wanted comfort snacks. I prioritized rest. I returned to my books and audiobooks for moments of escape. I let the sun hit my face, even when I didn't feel like being seen.

Healing doesn't come only after you land the next job. It starts in the waiting.

There were moments in this journey that felt honestly hopeless. Some weeks, there were no leads, no interviews, not even rejections. There was just silence. It is in that silence that you start to wonder if you're the only one struggling, and if something's wrong with *you*. I was lucky, very lucky, to have the support of my husband, who was both emotionally present and financially stabilizing. His pep talks, his sense of humor, and the little outings we did together helped pull me out of some dark moments. Knowing we had a second income meant we weren't in a full financial crisis, but I still carried the fear that nothing new was coming.

To cope, I broke my personal care into three categories:

1. Physical health

2. Mental and emotional health

3. Personal development through upskilling

Physical health was about movement. I aimed to get in some form of daily activity, with either a gym workout with weights or a long outdoor walk. I didn't do a lot of cardio (I probably should have!), but I leaned into walking for both physical benefit and mental release. Those walks became sacred time. They pulled me away from screens, from job boards, from resume tweaks and LinkedIn scrolling. They helped me clear my head. I'm lucky to live near some beautiful public trails and parks. Many mornings, I'd head out early before the rest of the world was moving, and just breathe. Sometimes the walks were with my dog. Sometimes I was alone. I was always grateful for that quiet space.

Alongside movement, I made a consistent effort to eat nourishing meals at home, drink plenty of water, and prioritize sleep. I'm not perfect with my diet. There was certainly some comfort snacking in the mix, but I stayed mostly grounded in simple, good-quality foods.

Mental and emotional health requires just as much intention. In addition to the walks, I reached out to friends and made time for conversations that had nothing to do with job searching. I also leaned into fiction audiobooks. These were stories that let me escape my current reality and gave my mind something else to focus on. It was a simple but effective form of mental hygiene. Even though I wasn't in financial peril, I still carried a heavy mental load. Every day brought that lingering anxiety of "what if this lasts even longer?" Having tools to decompress made a huge difference.

Then, finally, there was my own upskilling. I carved out time, which was usually about an hour a day, to build and improve digital content skills tied to the small business I'd been nurturing on the side. I dove into creating videos, managing my YouTube channel, designing digital courses, and expanding my social media presence. From the outside, I know it might have looked frivolous, but it wasn't. For the business I was trying to grow, visibility and digital credibility mattered. I was still very much a beginner, but I committed to learning anyway.

Here's what surprised me the most. These self-directed skills started generating small client opportunities. Women in my age range, many of them launching similar businesses, began reaching out. They wanted guidance on how to start a podcast, build a website, or create video content. I wasn't an expert, but I was a safe person they could ask. A few even paid me. Not a lot, but enough to remind me: nothing we learn is wasted. Those skills, and that confidence, are coming with me into whatever's next.

## Diversifying Your Income Streams

One of the most valuable lessons I learned was the importance of not relying on just one income stream. In the year leading up to my layoff, I had started a small side hustle. Initially, it was just a creative outlet, but something I didn't even realize I needed. As time went on, that little venture turned out to be incredibly beneficial. It brought in extra income, kept me productive, and helped expand my network in ways I hadn't anticipated.

It was my first experience with a portfolio career, which you learned about in Chapter 3. Having gone through job loss, I now have serious reservations about ever being dependent on just one income stream again. It doesn't mean I want to work myself into an early grave with an endless hustle. My side income streams do not add a ton of time to my week. I simply learned how to monetize some things I was already doing. People had long been coming to me for career transition advice, and I willingly gave it for free. Now I organized my delivery of that advice into a service-based coaching program, and I charge for the guidance I provide. It's the same effort, but there are dollars attached to it.

It's easy to feel like you're defined by the roles you've held for years. But stepping into entrepreneurship, even in a small way, forced me to think outside the box and discover new ways to use my skills. It was empowering to realize that I could create something of my own, build a brand, and offer services that people needed. It opened my eyes to new possibilities and gave me a sense of ownership over my future.

Being in midlife and having worked my way up to the executive level, my identity was deeply tied to that role. When I moved into this time of uncertainty, suddenly saying I *used* to be an executive didn't hold the same meaning anymore. I had to figure out who I was without the fancy job title and without belonging to a well-known organization. There was a bit of grieving and even some shame in that process. But ultimately, it pushed me to redefine myself. I learned to see my skills and experiences in a new light and realized that I could create something of my own that truly represented who I am.

## Embrace the Journey

Looking back on these months of job searching, I've come to realize that every challenge brings with it a lesson in resilience and growth. Whether it's understanding the power of a professional network, preparing for a longer-than-expected timeline, or prioritizing self-care and upskilling, each experience has shaped me in ways I never anticipated.

If you find yourself on a similar path, remember that you're not alone. Take the time to care for yourself, lean on your support network, and trust in your own ability to adapt and grow. Your journey may be unpredictable, but it is also rich with opportunities to discover new strengths and possibilities. As you move forward, know that every step you take is bringing you closer to the next exciting chapter of your life.

## Moving Forward: Your Turn to Thrive

If you find yourself in a season of uncertainty or transition, here are a few lessons you can take from my journey:

1. **Leverage Your Network**: Don't hesitate to reach out to your connections and let them know what you're looking for. Personal referrals can make all the difference.

2. **Embrace Lifelong Learning**: Invest in upskilling, whether it's digital skills, a new hobby, or even a side hustle. You never know how it might open doors for you.

3. **Redefine Your Identity**: Remember that you are more than your job title. Take the time to explore who you are beyond your professional role and discover new passions and strengths.

4. **Stay Resilient and Open-Minded**: Challenges can be opportunities in disguise. Stay open to new possibilities and trust that every step forward is part of your growth.

Your journey is uniquely yours, and each challenge you overcome brings you closer to the next exciting chapter of your life.

## Remember What You're Capable Of

I leaned into the creative work I had been building on the side. This was my podcast, my YouTube channel, my digital content. It started as an outlet. However, when the steady paychecks stopped, it became a lifeline.

I picked up small client projects. I said yes to speaking opportunities I would've ignored before. I started building my personal brand with intention.

Slowly, I remembered who I was.

You don't have to wait for someone to give you permission to be valuable. You already are.

## This Season Won't Last Forever

If you're in the thick of it right now, as a midlifer, newly unemployed and uncertain of what's next, please hear me: You are not broken. You are not behind. You are not alone.

The silence is hard. The rejection hurts. The doubt is heavy. But this season will not last forever.

Use it to get clear. Use it to heal. Use it to reconnect with what you love and what you're great at. If you can, use it to create something, anything, that proves to you that you still have something to offer. That's because you do.

## Turning Career Loss or Burnout Into a Personal Breakthrough

Let's be clear: starting over in midlife is not a failure. It's a flex. You didn't come this far just to settle. Yet, when the job ends, the burnout hits, or the title no longer fits, it can feel like you're staring down a blank page with no idea what to write next.

Here's what I know for sure: some of your most powerful pivots will begin with loss.

For me, it was a layoff. For you, it might be a toxic boss. Maybe the job you used to love now feels like a cage. When your identity is built on your title, all of it is gone when the job disappears.

Whatever brings you here, the question isn't "Why is this happening?" The real question is: What are you going to do with it?

## The End of Something Is the Beginning of You

One of the hardest things about midlife transitions is that they often arrive without your permission. You didn't plan to start over at 47. You didn't expect to be rebuilding your confidence at 53. You definitely didn't think you'd be learning how to reintroduce yourself to the world in your 50s. But here you are, still standing. You are still talented and so full of possibilities.

So let's drop the shame and pick up the pen. You get to write what happens next.

## Reframe: You're Not Behind, You're Recalibrating

Starting over doesn't mean going backward. It means starting from experience. Midlife job seekers bring something that no certificate or degree can offer: lived wisdom. You know how to work with people. You know what burnout feels like, and how to avoid it. You know your values. You've learned the hard way what kind of environments crush you and which ones help you thrive.

This isn't a reset. It's a recalibration.

## What Burnout Taught Me About Alignment

I'll never forget the moment I realized I was done. No, I wasn't just tired or annoyed. I was for real, done-done. What used to challenge me now drained me. What used to inspire me now made me roll my eyes. I had built a successful career, but it no longer fit the woman I had become.

That wasn't a breakdown. It was a breakthrough. Burnout became my breadcrumb trail. Every frustration pointed me toward something I had outgrown. Every drained Sunday night pointed to a value that was being ignored. It was time to pivot. That's how this book, this business, and this message were born.

**You Can Grieve AND Grow**

Let's normalize this: starting over in midlife can come with grief. You might feel grief for the years spent in the wrong role. There will be grief for the dream job that didn't turn out like you hoped. You might grieve for the version of you that stayed too long out of fear or loyalty.

But that grief? It's not weakness. It's proof that you've lived, loved, and cared. Now, you get to take what you've learned and move forward differently.

**What To Do When You're Laid Off in Midlife: A Practical Guide to Reclaiming Your Confidence and Creating a Plan**

So, what do you actually *do* when the job disappears? After the shock wears off, the silence sets in, and the reality hits your bank account, how do you respond?

Below are the steps I wish someone had handed me on a checklist. I hope they bring you clarity, power, and a little bit of peace.

**1. Give Yourself 48 Hours to Feel It**

Layoffs hit different in midlife. You've poured years, likely decades, into a career, a title, and a rhythm. When that's taken away, it's not just about income. It's emotional. Take two days to feel everything: the fear, the anger, the relief, the confusion. Journal, cry, sit still, and talk it out. Then, after those 48 hours, you will begin your plan.

## 2. File Immediately for What You're Owed

- **Severance** – Review any paperwork and understand the terms.

- **Unemployment** – Apply right away, even if you're optimistic about finding work quickly.

- **Health Insurance** – Look into COBRA, ACA options, or your spouse's coverage (if applicable).

Do not wait. These benefits exist for this exact moment. You paid into them. Let them support you.

## 3. Audit Your Finances (Without Shame)

Look at:

- Your essential expenses

- Any recurring subscriptions or services to pause or cancel

- Your emergency savings or other income streams

Create a lean but livable budget. If you have a partner or spouse, do this together to avoid silent assumptions or pressure.

## 4. Update Your Materials Like It's a Priority

This includes:

- Resume

- LinkedIn profile

- Professional bio

- Personal branding statement (who you are and what value you bring)

Your materials should reflect the level of wisdom and experience you have, not just tasks you've done, but outcomes you've delivered.

## 5. Don't Job Search Alone

Reach out to:

- Former colleagues
- Industry peers
- LinkedIn contacts
- People you've mentored or supported

Let them know you're in transition. Ask for conversations, not job openings. Referrals and opportunities often come from unexpected places, but only if people know you're available.

## 6. Spend No More Than 40% of Your Time on Job Boards

Online applications are convenient, but they can be a black hole. Shift your energy toward:

- Informational interviews
- Networking events (even virtual ones)
- Webinars or conferences in your industry
- Volunteering your skills where possible
- Put your name and face back in circulation.

## 7. Maintain a Routine

Wake up at the same time each day. Set "work hours" for your job search. Build in:

- Daily movement (walks, yoga, gym)
- Screen breaks
- Healthy meals

- Connection with friends or family
- Something that brings you joy (books, crafts, nature, prayer)

Having a daily structure will preserve your sanity. This is not a random euphemism when I mention preserving your sanity. I mean this literally.

## 8. Work on a Personal Project or Passion

This can be:

- A blog
- A business idea
- An online course
- Freelance work
- Creative writing

Don't wait to be picked. Midlife is your time to create something that belongs only to you.

## 9. Remind Yourself: You Are Not Your Job Title

Who you are doesn't disappear with a layoff. Midlife is proof that you've already survived hard things. This season is not a dead end. It's a redirect.

## 10. Stay Open to a Life You Didn't Plan For

This transition might hurt, but it might also lead you somewhere better. Stay open to new industries, flexible roles, short-term contracts, and even entrepreneurship. You never know what door this detour is opening.

## Quick Affirmation:

"I am not broken. I am being redirected. I still have value. I still have vision. I still have a future."

# PART TWO

## HOME

# CHAPTER 7

## The House Is Too Big, So Is the Burden: Why downsizing can be the most radical act of self-care

Homeownership has long been considered a badge of success, especially in Black communities. That big house in a good neighborhood? That was the dream. To pay off the mortgage and live debt-free one day? For years, that singular goal genuinely worked for us. After generations of Black people were systemically denied any wealth-earning opportunities within institutions and policies of racism, being able to own a house was the only option available for a long while. It was a right our grandparents and parents were damn proud to have. I won't downplay this fact one bit. Owning a house as a black person in America was a big deal.

But midlife has a funny way of shifting your perspective. The same home that once felt like a blessing began to feel like a burden. We had too much space, too much maintenance, and too many weekend hours eaten up by chores instead of joy. We realized we were spending more time *managing* our lifestyle than *living* it.

### What Downsizing Really Gave Us

We started looking into downsizing all of it. Downsizing wasn't just about square footage. It was about reclaiming our time, energy, and peace. When we let go of the house, we also let go of a long list of obligations: yard work, property taxes, HOA fees, and the endless to-do list that came with homeownership.

But we gained so much more:

- We gained freedom.

- We gained spontaneity.

- We gained a lifestyle that finally matched who we had become—not who we used to be.

Our new home is smaller, yes, but our life feels infinitely bigger.

## The Self-Care No One Talks About

You hear a lot about bubble baths and journaling as self-care, but you know what else is self-care? Letting go of a house that no longer serves you. Walking away from the emotional and financial weight of a property you've outgrown. Making bold choices that prioritize your mental clarity over maintaining appearances. Downsizing is one of the most radical and liberating acts of midlife self-care because it challenges everything we've been taught about success and permanence.

As more Americans enter midlife and beyond, the decision to downsize isn't just about shedding square footage. It's about reshaping life around what truly matters. According to a 2023 study published in the *Journal of Housing Economics*, many retirees and older adults are choosing to downsize not just for financial reasons, but also to improve their overall quality of life. The research found that individuals often relocate to smaller, more manageable homes in neighborhoods that better match their evolving needs, such as walkability, access to services, and community engagement (Best & Kleiner, 2023). This shift reflects a growing awareness that midlife is less about holding onto the big house and more about curating a lifestyle that offers peace, freedom, and alignment with one's current values.

We were no different. There wasn't one specific morning when we woke up and suddenly decided to sell our house. The decision to downsize unfolded slowly, over countless weekends spent on home maintenance, quiet dinners at a too-large table, and deep, late-night conversations about what we truly wanted from this next season of life.

After raising two boys in a spacious, suburban home that we had renovated to near perfection, the idea of leaving it behind felt both unthinkable and yet inevitable. Every room held memories, from birthday parties to holiday mornings to simple family rituals that shaped our days. But once the kids left for college, the house began to feel more like a museum than a home. It was beautiful, but no longer necessary.

Let me just say this right off the bat: I loved our house. I loved the way it wrapped around us like a custom-fit memory. The kitchen? Chef's kiss and custom-designed by yours truly. The hosting space? Immaculate. The yard? Magazine-ready. My husband might tell you he did most of the yard work, but don't let him fool you. I coordinated the vibe, okay? That house was good to us. But at some point, we had to admit: we were living in a shrine to a season that had already passed.

The kids were gone. Like, gone-gone. Dorm-room living, text-you-when-they-need-something, grown-folks-business gone. So suddenly we were staring at four bedrooms, multiple living spaces, a two-car garage, and a sea of stuff that made sense for who we used to be, not who we were becoming.

There's something funny that happens around 50. You start waking up one day, realizing you've been making choices for everybody else your whole life. Where to live? What's the best school for the kids? What kind of car? Will it fit the sports gear? Vacation? What can we afford between tuition and braces? Then suddenly, it's just...you. The other adult you chose to build this life with, who may or may not also be blinking at you like, "Wait, who are we without carpools and Saturday Target runs?"

For us, it started as a whisper. A little "what if" that we dared to say out loud. What if we sold the house? What if we let go of this place that had been the backdrop of our parenting, our parties, our projects, our peace? What if we chose a lifestyle that reflected our needs now?

At first, it felt like blasphemy. There was no talking about this with our extended family, because it felt like a deeply personal decision others might not understand. We were raised to believe that homeownership is the goal, the investment, the legacy. You work hard, buy the house, pay it off, and die there. That's the plan. That's the respectable grown-folk blueprint. We had followed it faithfully.

Until we didn't. We didn't have a midlife crisis. We had a midlife awakening. The house, as beautiful, functional, and Pinterest-worthy as it was, no longer fit the life we were ready to live.

So we got to work. By 'work,' I mean we created a spreadsheet. You think I'm joking, but listen: Overly organized, type A traits run this household. We crunched numbers. We compared costs. We had late-night debates about elevators and pet deposits. We toured high-rises and Googled phrases like "can you be too old to rent an apartment downtown." (Spoiler: you cannot.)

Then we did something that still makes my husband twitch: we sold almost everything we owned.

Furniture, appliances, and decor that had been carefully curated over the years to say, "This family has it together". We made a website. It was a literal digital showroom. I took pictures of every last item and priced it like a going-out-of-business sale. Yes, honey, we moved the product, and fast.

Friends pulled up with trucks and their PayPal ready to transact. Items disappeared within minutes. My husband still looks at me sideways about a certain living room set that I may or may not have let go for the price of a good bottle of wine. He mourned. I exhaled. Every piece that left the house was one less thing to worry about.

We had spent years accumulating, upgrading, and investing. Now we were divesting. It was on purpose and done joyfully. With a little nervous laughter and a whole lot of faith, we cleared the house and kept roughly one-third of all its contents.

The day we closed the door on that house for the last time, we felt everything all at once. Gratitude. Grief. Excitement. Nerves. But mostly, we felt light. It was not just physical (although our movers could tell you about that miracle), but also emotional. I'll add spiritual and a bit existential, too. We had let go of the thing we were taught to value above all else in order to prioritize peace.

Our apartment? Oh, it's gorgeous. We gained downtown views, an on-property gym, and pool we don't have to maintain. There's a 24-hour concierge who knows my dog by name. The best part? We walk everywhere. This includes when we go to brunch, to concerts, or to that one coffee shop with the spicy chai latte that I swear changes lives. It feels like freedom.

Do I miss having a garage? Sure, when I'm trying to figure out where my car is parked. Do I miss hosting big holiday parties? Sometimes, but not as much as I love showing up to someone else's party and leaving without doing dishes.

We traded space for spontaneity. We offloaded stuff for stories. We gave up a mortgage for mobility.

Let me tell you: I have never felt more grown.

This pivot isn't for everyone, and that's okay. But if you're staring at a home that feels more like a museum than a sanctuary, or if you're spending your weekends maintaining a lifestyle you're no longer living, then maybe it's time to ask yourself something. What could this next chapter look like, if you dared to write it differently? Because sometimes, the bravest thing you can do is let go of what once fit you perfectly, so you can finally grow into what fits you now.

**Embracing the Melanated Midlife Mindset**

Embracing the 'Melanated Midlife Mindset' means recognizing that midlife is a time of profound transformation and empowerment. At this stage in life, we've accumulated a wealth of experience and wisdom that uniquely positions us in the professional world and in our personal lives. We understand ourselves better than ever, and we have the clarity to know what we truly want.

This is also the time when our earning potential is at its peak. In addition, we need to be unapologetically clear about our financial goals. Money is a crucial part of designing the life we want, and it's important to have honest conversations about what we need financially. By understanding and articulating our financial needs, we empower ourselves to pursue opportunities that truly align with our desired lifestyle. Money might not buy happiness, but it does give us the freedom and flexibility to live the life we envision.

By embracing all of these elements, we can step confidently into this new chapter of our lives, fully empowered and ready to thrive.

Now, let's turn the focus to you. Embracing the Melanated Midlife Mindset means being honest and intentional about what you truly want in this next chapter of your life. Take a moment to reflect:

- What are the goals that you're aiming for?

- What does your ideal life look like?

- Think about what truly excites you and what you might be ready to let go of.

Remember, you're not here because you're unsatisfied or ungrateful for where you are now, but because you're ready for what comes next. Allow yourself to dream boldly and be clear about your aspirations. This is your time to design a life that truly reflects who you are and what you desire.

## Reflect Before You Redesign

Before you get swept up in moving quotes and furniture donations, take a beat to reflect on what's actually prompting the desire to downsize. This isn't just about real estate. It's about identity, purpose, and freedom.

Ask yourself:

- What parts of your home life feel like joy? What parts feel like an obligation?

- If you weren't worried about what others might say, what kind of home would truly support your lifestyle now?

- What are you afraid to let go of, and what might that fear be costing you?

- If you had no emotional ties to your current home, would you choose it again?

- What kind of daily life do you crave in this season of your life?

## So, How Did We Do It? Practical Steps to Downsize Your Life

Once we made the decision to move, we didn't just toss out some furniture and call it a day. We got strategic. This wasn't just about relocating. It was about redefining our lifestyle. Here's what it actually looked like in real life, not just on a checklist.

## 1. Create a Timeline (and Add Cushion)

We didn't wake up one day and throw a "For Sale" sign on the lawn. This was a slow build. Quiet conversations over dinner. Middle-of-the-night "what ifs" whispered into pillows. Truth is, even when it looked like a fast move to everyone else, we'd been mentally preparing for several months.

We mapped out our move like a mini project plan. But we also padded that plan with a margin. Life happens. Emotions bubble up.

Schedules shift. We gave ourselves the grace of time, and I'd urge you to do the same. Six months is a great starting point, especially if you need to sell your home or purge decades of stuff. Rushing leads to stress, and midlife pivots should feel intentional, not frenzied.

## 2. Do the Math

Let me be honest: we almost backed out when we first compared rent prices to our mortgage. On paper, it looked like we were about to spend *more* to get *less*. But that was before we sat down and calculated everything: the HOA dues, property taxes, the sky-high summer electric bills (our highest was over $700), yard maintenance, pest control, roof repairs, and all the other "invisible" costs that come with homeownership.

Once we added those up, we realized we were already paying luxury prices to live in the suburbs, without any of the fun. Our new downtown apartment came with amenities like a gym, pool, concierge, and valet parking. We weren't losing money. We were finally spending it on *us*.

## 3. Start the Decluttering Early

This was the part that took the most out of us, physically and emotionally. We had stuff. Beautiful stuff. Sentimental stuff. Duplicate stuff. Stuff we forgot we owned.

Every weekend, we picked a room and went in with a goal: keep, sell, donate, or discard. If we hadn't touched it in a year, we seriously questioned if it deserved a spot in our future. We didn't want to bring clutter into our next chapter. We were ruthless and tender at the same time. I spent moments laughing at old photo albums, gently parting with our kids' school projects, giving our furniture new homes with friends and neighbors.

By the time moving day came, we had lightened our load by nearly two-thirds, and I haven't missed a single thing we let go.

### 4. List Your Non-Negotiables

Downsizing doesn't mean settling. It means being crystal clear on what matters most. We weren't just looking for an apartment. We were designing a lifestyle. So we made a list.

We wanted walkability. We wanted to be close to live music venues, great food, and coffee shops. We needed a secure building with a 24-hour concierge. Of course, we couldn't live without a space that welcomed our dog (who has more attitude than most people, by the way).

We weren't willing to compromise on those things. So when we toured spaces, we knew within five minutes if it was a yes or a no. Having that clarity saved us from decision fatigue. It reminded us that this move was for *us*, not for resale value, not for status, and definitely not for other people's opinions.

### 5. Do a Test Drive of Your New Life

Before we signed anything, we spent our weekends in the area we were considering. We pretended we already lived there. We grabbed coffee at local spots. We walked the sidewalks. We timed the drive to the grocery store. We sat on patios and people-watched.

That kind of trial run gave us a real sense of how our days could feel in the new space. It also helped us confirm whether the vibe was right. Could we picture ourselves here? Did the energy of the neighborhood match the lifestyle we were after? Test driving your new life before you commit is one of the smartest things you can do, and one of the most fun.

### 6. Talk About the Emotional Side

No one talks about the grief that comes with a joyful decision. I did not cry when we signed the lease to our new place. However, I quietly sobbed a little when I closed the door to our old home for the last time.

It wasn't sadness, exactly. It was gratitude. It was the full weight of every holiday, scraped knee, first day of school, late-night talk, and quiet Sunday that had happened within those walls. So I gave myself permission to walk through slowly. I thanked each room. I took pictures. I paused.

Downsizing is more than logistics. It's letting go of the stage where you performed your life for so many years. Give yourself room to grieve. Then, my dear, you will welcome the new.

### 7. Plan for the Pivot, Not Just the Move

Our move wasn't just a change of address. It was a realignment of priorities. That meant we had to think beyond the move-in date. What did we want our lives to look like in this next season?

My husband signed up for classes at a local university for an intense certification he'd always wanted to pursue. I found more time for creative projects, spontaneous events, and connecting with friends in ways I couldn't when my weekends were full of parent booster committee meetings and Home Depot runs.

This wasn't just a relocation. It was a reinvention. We didn't just plan for the move. We planned for what would bloom *after* the move. That's what made it worth it.

### Your Downsizing Game Plan: A Midlife Reset Checklist

If this chapter sparked something in you (or maybe a curiosity before a full-on "I'm ready"), then let's make it real. Here's a simplified checklist pulled straight from our own process and the workbook we created to help others walk this path.

### Clarify Your Why

- What do you want more of: freedom, travel, simplicity?
- What are you tired of managing, fixing, or justifying?

## Know Your Numbers

- Compare current home expenses vs. new living options.
- Factor in hidden costs: lawn care, taxes, utilities.
- Don't just think about money saved. Consider energy gained.

## Declutter with Intention

- Tackle one room at a time.
- Use the Keep / Sell / Donate / Discard method.
- Photograph sentimental items. Let go with gratitude.

## Choose Your Next Nest with Care

- Make a non-negotiable list: walkability? concierge? pet-friendly?
- Tour neighborhoods and buildings at different times of day.
- Trust your gut, and your spreadsheet.

## Prep for the Emotional Side

- Say goodbye to each space on your terms.
- Capture the memories, not just the things.
- Talk openly with your partner or family about what this move means.

## Handle the Logistics Like a Boss

- Hire movers if you can. You deserve rest.
- Sell items via a Google Site or Facebook Marketplace.
- Notify your inner circle and start prepping early.

**Embrace the New Chapter**

- Celebrate your pivot.

- Host a toast in your new space, even if it's just takeout and wine.

- Stay curious about what else can change now that you have taken this big step.

# CHAPTER 8

## You Don't Owe Anyone a Mortgage: Releasing the "Forever Home" Fantasy and Choosing Flexibility Instead

There's this unspoken expectation a lot of us internalized somewhere between college graduation and our first big promotion: that to be grown, responsible, and successful, we needed to own a home. I don't mean just any home, but a *forever* home. It had to be something big enough to host the holidays, impress your parents, and fit all the dreams your younger self scribbled in a journal somewhere. The house was supposed to be the reward, the arrival and the ultimate adult flex.

For a long time, I believed that too. I did the whole homeownership dance. We purchased the starter home, made upgrades, and carried out renovations. We didn't take a honeymoon after our wedding because we funneled all our money into that first down payment. I remember the pride I felt when designing the kitchen just the way I wanted it, choosing the backsplash and lighting fixtures as if I were curating a magazine spread. I played hostess at birthdays, holidays, and family dinners that looked like they belonged in a Pottery Barn catalog. I was proud of our home. It was warm, welcoming, and full of love. Then, eventually, something shifted.

When our sons each prepared to leave for college, the house felt different. It didn't feel like an accomplishment anymore. It felt more empty and more like a burden. It was too much space for two people who were no longer entertaining a house full of teenagers. I'd walk past rooms that sat barren for weeks. The energy bills kept climbing. The yard work that once brought my husband joy became a sweaty chore he dreaded. Every repair, every maintenance task, every HOA notification began to feel like a weight. The dream no longer fit the life we were living. Once we stopped trying to ignore that fact, it became impossible to pretend.

So we let it go. We sold the house. Sold most of the furniture. Let go of the dining room table that once seated the whole family, and the backyard grill station, which we only used for parties. We walked away from a mortgage we could easily afford, but emotionally couldn't carry anymore. We did something people rarely talk about with joy in midlife: we chose to rent.

Now, let me be clear. This wasn't some last-resort, "we have no other option" move. It was an intentional, joyful decision rooted in a deep desire for ease. Renting gave us the flexibility we craved. We wanted no HOA drama and no $700 summer utility bills (yes, you read that correctly). We wanted no roof leaks to patch or flower beds to mulch. We moved into a right-sized apartment in the middle of the city, surrounded by culture, food, green spaces, and walkability. Our gym is on-site. Package deliveries are secured. Do we worry about repairs? That is someone else's problem. We reclaimed our weekends as ours again.

The honest truth is, yes, the rent is higher than our old mortgage. That's not to be glossed over. However, so was the cost of our peace when we were shackled to a house we no longer wanted. Sometimes owning something doesn't make you feel secure. It makes you feel stuck. What's the point of equity if the lifestyle that comes with it is draining you?

The idea that homeownership is the ultimate symbol of stability is being redefined by a growing number of midlifers who are opting out of the mortgage hustle. A 2024 survey by Bank of America found that 84% of baby boomer renters actively prefer renting over owning, citing reasons like freedom from maintenance, fewer financial burdens, and greater lifestyle flexibility. This isn't just about affordability. It's about intentional living.

Business Insider reported in 2025 that even affluent older adults are increasingly choosing to rent, reallocating what would have been their home equity into more liquid investments, such as stocks or business ventures. According to a 2024 Aspen Institute report, renter households actually saw a 43% increase in net worth between 2019 and 2022, surpassing homeowners in some cases, by leveraging pandemic-era savings and income supports to build diversified portfolios. For many in midlife, letting go of the "forever home" fantasy isn't giving up. It's leveling up.

I'm not here to bash homeownership. If it still fits your life, your needs, and your vision for the future, then by all means, keep it. There's nothing inherently wrong with owning a home. We enjoyed homeownership for two and a half decades. But here's what I want to say. The thing I wish someone had whispered in my ear 10 years ago: You don't owe anyone a mortgage. You no longer have to live up to your parents' expectations. It might not be the ideal image you still want. You don't have to keep living up to your younger self's checklist.

You owe yourself freedom. Flexibility. Space to pivot, rest, and dream new dreams.

Think about all the hidden costs that go along with owning a home. Sure, you're paying the mortgage, but what about the insurance? What about the HOA fees, maintenance, and repairs? How about pest control and seasonal upkeep? In Houston, we had flood insurance, windstorm insurance, and all the "just in case" coverage that came with living in a region prone to storms. We had already replaced the roof, renovated the bathrooms, and gutted the kitchen. Yet still, things kept breaking. This is because that's what houses do. They require care, attention, and money, even when they look beautiful on the outside.

I started calling them phantom costs. Those are things that don't appear on your monthly budget, but somehow keep draining your account. Our experience included a water heater leak in the attic that caused the ceiling in our bedroom to collapse in the middle of the night. More than once, our AC unit would quit in the middle of the hot summer months. We had a dishwasher that wouldn't drain. All those "surprises" tend to hit at the worst possible moment.

Now ask yourself: if you didn't have to deal with any of that, where would that money go? Would you travel more? Would you save more or pay down debt? Would you start that side hustle or invest in a creative project? Would there be time to support causes you care about? Could you take better care of yourself? The dollars aren't just about bills. They're about your bandwidth.

It's not always just the money. It's also your time, your energy, and your weekends. Think about where your Saturdays go right now. Are you living your life, or managing your house? My husband used to love tending to the lawn. Neighbors would compliment the curb appeal. But over time, that joy turned into dread. The Texas sun wasn't cute anymore. We weren't in our 30s. That pride turned into physical exhaustion, and eventually, a landscaping bill, because his time became more valuable than the compliments.

Even if you're outsourcing yard work and home repairs, you're still managing it, or scheduling it, and paying for it. You are carrying it in your mental load. That's energy you could be spending building the life you actually want to live. I hear more and more midlifers talking about wanting to travel, to experience the world, and to savor life. But you can't do that if you're stuck at home waiting for a plumber or painting the guest bedroom for the third time in five years.

Now, some folks will say, "Well, I'll just build new. That way everything's done." I totally get that. But even new homes come with problems. Things will settle. Materials will wear. Appliances will age. Unless you've got a crystal ball and a toolbox, you're still going to be spending time or money, or both.

For us, renting created room to breathe. We chose a community that had the kind of amenities we wanted. This was access to a gym, a pool with a deck, grocery deliveries, and security. We wanted a more mature vibe. That doesn't mean clubs and rooftop ragers, but quiet evenings and neighborly peace. We found exactly that, and we feel good about it every single day.

Listen, this could look totally different for you. Maybe you want to live near the water, or near your grandkids, or in a smaller town with a slower pace. Maybe you're single and thinking about co-living or getting a roommate to build community. Whatever your dream is, own it. Because the only thing you "owe" at this stage is a life that feels good to wake up to. I often daydream about a future where me and a few of my girlfriends grow old together in a house with separate suites and shared wine nights. It's silly, maybe, but it's mine. Plus, it makes me smile.

If you're still not sure what your next chapter could look like, try this. Take out a sheet of paper, or your phone, and just dream. What would your ideal midlife look like in the next five to ten years? How would you spend your mornings? Your money? Your energy? Who would you be with? Where would you live? Then ask yourself: Can I have that life in my current home?

If the answer is no, it might be time to get curious. What would need to shift? What could you let go of? What would it feel like to walk away from the stress, the debt, the leaks, the ladders, and the lawns?

Let's go back to the night our water heater leaked. It was in the attic above our bedroom (because of course it was), and we woke up to the sound of water trickling through the ceiling. By the next morning, part of it had collapsed. I looked at my husband, and I saw the weariness on his face. It wasn't panic, but bone-deep fatigue. He didn't say it out loud, but I knew the thought that was sitting heavy on his chest: "What's going to break next?" That was the moment. We needed a different kind of life. Now, when something breaks, I submit a ticket and go back to my coffee. That's the peace we bought when we sold the house.

So, let me leave you with this: You don't owe anyone a mortgage. You don't owe anyone the emotional labor of keeping up the dream. You don't owe your parents, your friends, or even your past self the fantasy of a house that no longer fits your life. You owe yourself joy, and that might look like simplicity. You deserve rest, and you have options.

This season of life is about upgrading every part of it. That includes your home, career, relationships, and wellness. Sometimes the biggest upgrade starts with letting go of what no longer serves. So I encourage you to be bold. Be selfish. Design the life you want, whether it includes a mortgage or not.

### Rethinking Wealth: Beyond the Four Walls

For so long, we were told that buying a home was *the* way to build wealth. Our parents taught us that a mortgage was a milestone. That equity building was your legacy. Yes, for many, it can be. But it's not the *only* way. In this season of life, it may no longer be the *best* way for you. For the record, I am not advocating that everyone give up on homeownership. You do you, boo. All I am saying is that you have options that extend beyond home ownership.

Wealth isn't just about owning property. It's about owning your time. It's about having choices. It's about freedom of movement, freedom from stress, and the freedom to say yes to things that light you up without worrying about the roof caving in, literally or figuratively.

When we let go of our house, we didn't stop building wealth. We just redefined how. We doubled down on retirement contributions. We paid off lingering debt. We invested in experiences, in wellness, and in relationships. We bought back our evenings and weekends. We created a margin.

Here's the thing: wealth also looks like rest. It looks like not spending your Saturday on a ladder or your savings on a new AC unit. It looks like affording joy without asking for permission. You can build wealth through stocks, IRAs, side businesses, angel investing, short-term rentals, high-yield savings, and yes, by simply spending less and enjoying more.

You don't have to tie your financial future to a piece of property that drains you. You can build a life of abundance in other ways. The goal is not just equity in a house. The goal is equity in *yourself*, in your peace, your possibilities, and your power to choose differently now that you know better.

**What About You?**

By now, you've heard our story, about how we went from holding tight to the dream of homeownership to letting it go in pursuit of something lighter, freer, and more aligned with who we are today. This chapter isn't really about us. It's about you.

Maybe you're sitting in a home that once fit your life perfectly but now feels more like a to-do list than a retreat. Maybe you're staring at a garage full of "just in case" items and wondering why you're still holding onto things you haven't touched in years. Or maybe you're still fully in love with your home, but you feel a little tug, a little curiosity, about what it might mean to live differently in this next chapter.

You don't have to make any big decisions today. You don't have to post your house on Zillow or tour apartments tomorrow. What you *can* do is start telling yourself the truth. Start examining the truth about how your home makes you feel, and what it's costing you to maintain. That means not just financially, but mentally, emotionally, spiritually, and about the dreams you've quietly pushed down to keep the status quo in place.

Then ask yourself: Is the dream still mine?

You're allowed to want something new. You're allowed to admit that what once felt like an achievement now feels like an anchor. You're allowed to dream about downsizing, renting, co-living, traveling, or completely starting over. You're allowed to do it without shame, guilt, or the need to explain it to anyone. This next part of the chapter is for you. It's your turn to reflect, get honest, and explore your relationship with homeownership. You don't need all the answers. You just need a willingness to ask yourself better questions.

## A Midlife Reflection on Space, Status, and Self-Fulfillment

This isn't about shaming homeownership or glorifying renting. This is about checking in. Check with yourself and with your season. Check in with your truth. This is about permission. Give yourself permission to pause and reevaluate. Give permission to dream differently. These questions are not just about where you live, but about *how* you live, *why* you live that way, and what you might be brave enough to want now.

Think of your home not just as a structure but as a mirror. What does it reflect back to you? Is it still aligned with your needs, your energy, your joy? Or are you holding onto something out of habit, fear, or someone else's version of success? Let's dig into some reflections to help you sort through what fits you best.

### Part 1: Releasing the Fantasy

Take a moment to explore the stories you've been carrying. Don't just think of the ones about square footage, but the ones about identity, safety, validation, and arrival.

**What messages were you raised with about homeownership and what it means to be successful?**

Was it the marker of stability? Of "making it"? Were you taught that renting meant you were irresponsible, or that you hadn't arrived yet? These beliefs often run deep, and we don't even realize how much they shape our choices until we pause to question them. Your definition of success is allowed to change.

**Did buying a home feel like something you truly *wanted*, or something you were *expected* to do?**

Be honest with yourself here. Was buying your home an act of self-fulfillment, or was it part of the unspoken checklist handed to you by your parents, your community, or society at large? Did you want the home? Or was it the feeling of being seen as someone who owned one?

**When you look around your current space, what feelings come up? Peace? Pride? Stress? Nostalgia? Guilt? All of the above?**

What does your home evoke emotionally? Are you holding onto rooms full of memories, or rooms full of obligations? Do you walk in the door and exhale, or does the to-do list hit you before you set your purse down? There's no shame in whatever truth rises up. Just observe it. That feeling is telling you something.

**Part 2: The Lifestyle Tradeoff**

This is where you start to imagine beyond what you've always done, because everything you're holding onto requires energy. In this season, energy is a limited resource.

**What might you gain emotionally, financially, or physically by downsizing or letting go of ownership entirely?**

Think beyond the numbers. Could you reclaim your time, your creativity, your weekends? Could you afford therapy, travel, hobbies, or a housekeeper without the mortgage, taxes, or maintenance costs? Could your body feel better without the physical demands of upkeep?

**What are you afraid to lose if you let that go? And be honest. Is that fear rooted in fact, or just habit and perception?**

Are you worried about what people will say? That you'll look like you've taken a step backward? That you won't feel "settled"? Or is there a deeper fear, like being unmoored, or no longer being needed? Now ask: is that fear grounded in truth... or simply in the familiarity of the story you've been telling?

**What parts of your lifestyle are currently on pause, like travel, hobbies, rest, spontaneity, because your home requires so much of you?**

What's the cost of keeping things the same? Is it the trip you've been delaying? Maybe it's the nap you never take. It might be the creative spark you haven't explored. How about the Saturday brunches you skip because you're waiting on the plumber? If your house is costing you more than money, it may be time to reimagine your setup.

### Part 3: The Flexibility Forecast

This is where we drop the *shoulds*, silence the critics, and let you dream out loud. The version of you that's allowed to be *fully* selfish shows up here.

**If you could design your ideal living situation for the next 5 years, what would it look like? City or small town? Condo or co-living? Quiet or vibrant?**

Forget what's reasonable. What do you crave? Do you want walkability? Silence? More nature? Less space? More connection? Less isolation? What environment would support the version of you that is ready to emerge?

**What kind of housing setup would allow you to live more freely, whether that's traveling more, spending less, or having less to manage?**

Would a lock-and-leave setup open up time to see the world? Would renting free up the budget for a sabbatical or new career move? Would a smaller space make it easier to clean, maintain, and breathe? What would you do more of if your home stopped asking so much from you?

**What's stopping you from exploring that vision? Is the obstacle real... or just familiar?**

We often confuse comfort with safety. Are you staying in place because it's truly what you want, or just what you've always done? Is fear making the decisions? What might become possible if you took one small step toward something new?

**Try This Exercise: The Real Cost of Staying**

This is where clarity meets math. Let's break it down in black and white—and then listen for what you feel between the numbers.

1.  List every monthly and annual cost of your current home:

    o   Mortgage or loan payment

    o   Property taxes

    o   Insurance (homeowners, flood, wind, etc.)

    o   Utilities (electric, gas, water)

    o   Lawn care, pest control, security systems

    o   HOA fees

    o   Maintenance and repairs (average what you've spent over the last year)

2. Now, research the rent for a place in your desired area or lifestyle—maybe smaller, maybe more central, maybe with amenities you'd actually use.

3. Compare the numbers. Then go deeper:

   ○ What's the *emotional cost* of staying in your current home?

   ○ What's the *time cost*?

   ○ What would it feel like to let those responsibilities go—even if the price tag is similar?

# CHAPTER 9

## Let It Go So You Can Let It In: Decluttering in Midlife is the Most Emotional Makeover You'll Ever Do

L et's go ahead and tell the truth. This part is going to be hard. Decluttering in midlife isn't just about creating space. It's about sorting through years of your life in physical form. You're not just going through stuff. You're confronting memories, identities, and emotions that have been packed away in closets, drawers, and storage bins, sometimes for decades.

Most of us spent the first half of our adult lives accumulating. We bought houses and filled them. We bought matching dishware, throw pillows for every season, and outfits for bodies we no longer have or events we never attended. We kept every school picture, every art project, every homemade ornament with crooked googly eyes. We didn't just keep the item. We kept the emotion.

Why do we do this? A big part can be our sentimental attachment and nostalgia. Letting go of certain items can feel like erasing an important part of our history. We also might have a "just in case" mentality, where keeping things feels like a way to be prepared for the unexpected, even if the likelihood of needing those items is slim. Or maybe like so many of us Gen X kids, our identity and self-worth are attached to our material things. Downsizing can feel like a loss of status. It can signal that you are moving on from a chapter you are not ready to close. For me personally, all the purging felt like I was wasting money. Even though I might not have used some of those discarded items in years, it still initially felt like a financial failure.

When it came time for us to downsize, I found myself standing in the middle of it all, surrounded by boxes of memories. Some of the hardest items to go through were my kids' old photos. I had forgotten how many overpriced school portraits I ordered over the years. There was the wallet-sized, jumbo-sized, black-and-white, and sepia-toned (Lord, why did we do sepia?). There were Christmas program snapshots where they looked like baby angels in too-big costumes, and of course, the crap-tastic homemade Christmas ornaments made out of glitter, glue, and pure love. Let's not forget the Valentine's Day cards written in backward letters and held together with lopsided hearts and globs of Elmer's glue.

I didn't rush it. I let myself sit in those memories. I cried a little. I laughed a lot. I took pictures of the best stuff before letting it go. Revisiting all of those precious artifacts felt sacred, not because I needed to keep every scrap, but because I needed to honor the beautiful season those scraps represented.

That's what makes this work so layered. It is physical. Yes, your back might be sore from hauling bins and trash bags. But it's so emotional, too. Letting go of things that once mattered doesn't mean those memories don't still matter. It means you're making space. Space for what fits now. You are thoughtfully making space for ease and for joy.

You don't have to do it all in a weekend. You don't have to get it perfect. What you do have to do is start. Buried under all that stuff is a lighter, freer version of you, and they're ready to breathe.

So let's take it one drawer, one bin, one memory at a time.

**What decluttering really means when your identity is tied to your stuff**

There's a specific kind of weight that doesn't show up on a scale: the weight of unmade decisions, sentimental clutter, and outdated versions of yourself hiding in drawers and storage bins.

When I started decluttering for our midlife downsize, I thought I was just getting rid of things. I was wrong. What I was really doing was untangling myself from a lifetime of stories, roles, and expectations tied to those things. Let me tell you something. Real talk…some of those stories were holding me back.

**The Emotional Side of Decluttering: It's Not Just Stuff**

We don't just hold on to things because we're sentimental. We hold on to things because they were there during important moments. They *meant* something. That dress in the back of the closet? It's not just a dress. It might be the one you wore to your anniversary dinner before everything changed. The box of baby shoes in the attic? It's not about the shoes. It's about who you were when someone called you "mommy" every 15 minutes. Even the coffee mugs, the throw pillows, and the books from your career are all things. But those things make you remember how they made you feel, and who you were. That's the part we're really afraid to let go of.

In midlife, it's not unusual to feel like our identity is in transition. We've spent decades building lives that revolved around other people's needs: our children, our partners, our work. When the dust settles and the house quiets, we start to wonder, *Who am I now?* Sometimes our stuff feels like the only thing anchoring us to who we've been. And letting go? It feels like we are erasing ourselves.

But here's what I've learned. Your memories don't live in the objects. They live in you. The love you had, the life you lived, and the moments you shared will still be there. They don't disappear just because the item does.

So if you need to, pause when you pick up the wedding dress, or the kindergarten art project, or your grandmother's china. Say thank you. Say goodbye. Take a photo. Tell the story out loud to someone who will honor it with you. That's how you release the weight without losing the meaning. Letting go is not a betrayal of who you were. It's an offering to who you are becoming.

Once you understand that, once you feel the lightness that follows the grief, decluttering stops being about tidying up. It becomes a form of liberation.

According to a study by the UCLA Center on Everyday Lives of Families, excess physical clutter has been linked to increased stress levels and decreased focus. The human brain prefers order. Too much clutter literally stresses out your mind.

## Four Piles and a Breakthrough

During our move, I started with the usual categories: Keep, Donate, Sell, and Trash. But somewhere in the process, I added a fifth pile: Memorialize. This was because there were things I couldn't keep, but also couldn't just toss in the trash. My kids' kindergarten drawings, old awards, and photos I hadn't looked at in years, but suddenly couldn't stop crying over.

So instead of physically holding onto every object, I gave myself permission to hold onto the memory. I took pictures and made small digital albums. I created a keepsake box for each son with a few chosen items. I learned that honoring your past doesn't always require packing it into your future.

## The Closet: A Capsule of Your Former Selves

Let's talk about the closet. Oooh, child, that is where all my insecurities stand up and talk back to me. That was the hardest space of all. Not because of how much was in it, but because of what it all represented. I had clothes for three different body sizes, two past jobs, and a few versions of me that are now ancient history. I held onto blazers I hadn't worn since commuting to an office, heels I hadn't dared to put on since my last major conference, and jeans that belonged to a younger, skinnier me I was always promising to "get back to."

It wasn't just a wardrobe. It was a museum of unfinished business. So I started asking hard questions. Would I buy this again today? Who am I keeping this for? If the answer wasn't rooted in my current or future self, it had to go.

Let me be clear. This wasn't about shame. This was about alignment. I needed to see myself, honor who I was right now, and still choose to show up for who I'm becoming. I urge you to be careful not to slip down that slippery slope of more *shoulds*, and beat yourself up because those jeans don't fit anymore. You are not a failure or less worthy at a different size. You are evolving. Be grateful for every memory that bubbles up while you go through those old clothes. Those items supported you beautifully once upon a time. Give thanks for those moments and prepare to move forward.

## A Lighter Life Is a Fuller Life

Every time I let something go, whether it's a dress, a duplicate photo, or a coffee maker I hadn't used in two years, I felt a little lighter in the aftermath. The lightness was felt not just in my home. I had more mental energy. I experienced more emotional clarity. There were fewer distractions. I had less guilt and more room to dream.

With all the purging, I could look around our home and see less clutter. Our home became easier to clean, for sure. My thoughts became easier to sort, too. The mornings were less frantic. My closet was less confusing. My decisions were more intentional. There's power in that kind of space. Because once you let go of what no longer serves you, you're finally able to let in what's meant for you.

How many times have you been in a moment of irritability and uttered out loud, "I do not have time for this"? I can imagine you having one of those moments right now as you consider what it will take to begin your own decluttering project. It's not a little thing, but the payoff is huge. There is a theory called socioemotional selectivity, which suggests that as people age, they no longer prioritize material possessions.

Psychological studies confirm that people over 50 derive greater joy from experiences and relationships than from accumulating more things. Investing in memories rather than material goods leads to longer-term happiness. According to the Mayo Clinic, reducing mental and physical clutter lowers blood pressure, improves sleep, and enhances overall well-being. This means decluttering isn't just about space, it's about health.

## Action Steps: Declutter With Meaning

Decluttering isn't just about getting your space together. It's about getting *yourself* together. It's about choosing ease over expectation, alignment over accumulation. Each of these steps is designed to support your spirit, not just your square footage. Take what you need. Come back to them when you're ready. But know this: there is freedom waiting for you on the other side.

## 1. Name Your Why (Because "Just Because" Isn't Enough)

Start here. Before you touch a single drawer, ask yourself: *Why now?*

Why do you want to clear the clutter? What's calling you to create space?

Maybe you're tired of the constant mental weight. Maybe you're entering a new season—empty nesting, post-divorce, retirement, or reinvention—and your environment hasn't caught up to your growth. Whatever the reason, give it language. Write it down. Speak it out loud. Tape it to your mirror if you need to.

When you hit the emotional wall, and you will, your "why" will be the lifeline that keeps you moving forward.

## 2. Use the Four-Box Method (But Make It Sacred)

This isn't just organization. It's a ceremony. You're sorting through your life, and that deserves tenderness. Set up four categories as you move through your space:

- **Keep**: These are the items that align with your *present* self. They support your daily life, bring you joy, or reflect who you're becoming.

- **Donate**: These items are still useful, just not to *you*. Let them go with love, knowing they'll serve someone else's story now.

- **Sell**: This is for the things of value you no longer need. The high-end dress you never wore. The fancy kitchen appliance that never made it out of the box. You're not being wasteful. You're reclaiming your space *and* your money.

- **Trash**: Some things have simply reached the end of their journey. Let them go without guilt.

- **Memorialize**: This isn't exactly a box, but it might pop up as a big consideration. These are the hard-to-part-with items, like baby clothes, letters, and mementos. Take a photo. Write a memory. Create a digital keepsake or small curated box. The memory can stay. The object doesn't have to.

Set a timer if it helps. Turn on music. Light a candle. Make this process feel like care, not punishment. When the timer goes off and you've done as much as you can for that day, pause the work and pick up where you left off the next day.

### 3. Check Your Closet for Old Versions of You

Your closet is a time capsule. Often, it's holding on to identities you've already released. Take a real inventory of what's in there. Is it clothing for a body you no longer have? A job you no longer do? A´lifestyle you no longer live? Ask:

- Would I buy this again today?

- Who am I keeping this for?

- Do I feel good *right now* when I wear this?

Don't judge yourself. This is about alignment, not shame. You are not the same person you were ten years ago, and that's a blessing, my dear. Let your closet catch up to your evolution.

### 4. Try the "One-Year Rule" (With Compassion)

If you haven't worn it, touched it, used it, or even *thought about it* in a year… It's probably time to release it. This rule is not about scarcity. It's about honesty. We keep so much "just in case," but those cases rarely come. Be brave enough to let go of the hypothetical.

If it's too hard right now, then that's okay. Create a "maybe" bin. Label it with today's date. Revisit it in 90 days. Trust that your clarity will catch up with your courage.

### 5. Build Your Real Wardrobe First, Then Expand It With Intention

Instead of starting with what to let go of, begin with what to *keep*. Pull out the items you actually wear. The pieces that fit your body, your lifestyle, and your energy *now*. Hang them together. Stand back and look at what you've created.

This is your real wardrobe. These are your staples. From there, build out a capsule wardrobe, intentionally and slowly. Add quality, versatile pieces over time, not on impulse. Think less "trend" and more "timeless." Let getting dressed feel like an act of self-respect, not self-doubt.

## 6. Give Yourself Permission to Grieve and Celebrate

You're not just letting go of things. You're letting go of old roles, expired dreams, and identities that no longer fit. That means it will get emotional.

So when you find yourself sitting on the floor holding your kid's second-grade artwork, or a dress from your honeymoon, or your mama's chipped teacup, just breathe. You can cry or laugh. Take a picture. Write a memory. Then let it go, if you're ready. Clearing space doesn't mean forgetting the past. It means honoring it enough to move forward.

## 7. Be Kind to Your Body While You Clear Your Space

Decluttering is *physical* labor. Bending, lifting, reaching, and sorting will take a toll. Be kind to your midlife body while you tackle this project—stretch, hydrate, and schedule breaks. Don't try to conquer your whole house in one day. You're not on an HGTV show. This is real life. Do one drawer, one shelf, one closet at a time.

Set a timer for two hours max. When it goes off, stop. Rest. Celebrate what you did, instead of fixating on what's left. This is not a sprint. It's sacred work.

## 8. Don't Just Declutter. Reclaim

You are not doing this just to have fewer things. You're doing this to have *more life*. Your reward will be more space to think. You'llfeel more at ease in your routines. You will gain more permission to change and more clarity about what matters. There will be more room for the experiences, relationships, and dreams that are meant for this version of you.

So the next time you hesitate to let something go, ask yourself: *Is this item supporting the life I want... or the life I've already outgrown?*

Choose freedom. Choose peace. Choose the version of you that's waiting on the other side of the clutter.

**Reflection Prompts:**

1. What's one item in your home you're keeping out of guilt, not joy?

2. Which version of yourself do you still see reflected in the items around your home?

3. What does "letting it in" look like for you at this stage of life?

**Journal Exercises:**

- **Inventory Your Identity Items:** List 3-5 sentimental items that represent old versions of yourself. For each, ask:
    - "What memory or identity does this item hold?"
    - "Do I need this item to keep that memory alive?"
    - "Is there a way to honor it without keeping it physically?"

- **Your Midlife Room-by-Room Declutter Plan:** Choose one room. Write down:
    - What is your vision for this room in your next chapter?
    - What doesn't fit that vision anymore?
    - What will you do with each misaligned item? (Keep, Donate, Sell, Trash, Memorialize)

**Action Step:** Set a "Let Go" day on your calendar. Choose one category (photos, clothing, keepsakes, kitchen items) and commit to making progress with the four-pile method. Give yourself a stop time, and reward yourself afterward.

# CHAPTER 10

## The Kids Are Grown. Now What About You? Empty nesting as an invitation to rediscover your own joy

Nobody prepares you for the silence. After years of packed schedules, laundry piles, "What's for dinner?" questions, and chauffeuring your kids between school, sports, and social lives, one day it just… stops. You walk past the bedroom that's no longer messy. The fridge stays stocked longer. There's no backpack by the front door, no unexpected sleepovers, no last-minute school projects due tomorrow.

At first, the quiet feels like a reward. A deep exhale. But eventually, it becomes a question mark. What now? More honestly… who am I, now? My kids, who used to dominate the household with their activities, their friends hanging out, and all their mood swings, are now somewhere else full-time. Getting a phone conversation out of them is pretty nonexistent, and even receiving a response to a simple text message is like waiting for grass to grow in the desert. As the person formerly known as *mommy,* I am just another thing that faded into the background of their lives. They have reached their own main character season, and *mommy* has been relegated to a supporting role these days.

There are two dominant responses to empty nesting. There is role loss vs. role relief. Researchers at Stanford and UCLA found that the empty nest phase isn't one-size-fits-all. Some people feel a deep sense of role loss, while others experience relief and new emotional freedom. What you feel might depend on your personal history, your culture, and what you're walking into, not just what you're letting go of (Carstensen et al., 2024). That helped me feel less guilty about the emotional rollercoaster I was riding.

This, my friend, is the natural order of things when it comes to parenthood. If you stayed present and loving while protecting them from harm throughout their childhood, then you did your job well. If they grow into independent young adults who can set their own goals and figure out how to achieve them, then that is your ultimate flex. Stand up and take a bow. The progression of parenting is to raise them well enough that they no longer need you. Of course, we love having our adult children around, but not if they are still dependent on you for every dollar and decision. So when you reach this threshold of parenting and transition into a period when your grown kids are starting to stand on their own two feet, then you are ready to turn the focus back on you.

## The Role You Built Your Life Around

For so long, parenthood or general adulthood, dictated the rhythm of your life. Everything else, even your own dreams, got scheduled around it. It gave structure, purpose, and identity. But what happens when that role no longer needs you in the same way?

We don't talk enough about the identity shift that comes when our children become adults. In a 2024 concept analysis, researchers identified six major emotional shifts tied to empty nest syndrome: grief, silence, role disruption, identity erosion, adaptation, and eventual relief (Ahmadi Khatir et al., 2024). If you're feeling like you don't recognize your life anymore, you're not broken. You're transitioning.

We celebrate the launch, the independence, and the pride of watching them stand on their own. But we skip over the quiet grief, the disorientation, the invisible unraveling of a role you spent decades perfecting. For me, that grief hit me the hardest during the holidays. Remember, in our former suburban house, we took great pride in opening up our home for warm moments to gather with loved ones. Each year, my husband manually installed all the outdoor lights, and at my peak, I had 3 Christmas trees spread throughout the house, along with festive decorations in every room. Yes, I really do mean every room. We loved it, and I loved the response we got from friends and family when they came over for our annual Thanksgiving dinners and Christmas parties.

But when we moved on from that home, the big holiday bash traditions had to end. Our new apartment, as lovely as it was, truly was too small for hosting more than a couple of friends at a time. I did put up my Christmas tree and decorations, but the kids weren't home to appreciate it. Our home was very different without the holidays buzzing with people and activities, and I allowed myself to quietly grieve the change. The magical holiday traditions we were able to maintain for two decades were part of a bygone era. Now we just had memories. The kids had other places they wanted to be most of the time. Their social calendars weren't supervised by me anymore. It was time for me to process my grief over this loss and graciously move into this new chapter. The evolution had begun.

Research from the *Journal of Geriatric Mental Health* found that many midlife couples felt a sharp dip in satisfaction during this phase, not because they didn't love their new lives, but because cherished traditions and roles shifted so suddenly (2020). You're not just mourning a home. You're mourning the season it represented.

You're still their parent. That doesn't go away. However, as time passes, what's required of you changes. With that change, you're offered something unexpected: space. A fascinating study found that when adult children move out, especially after years of shared space, parents often experience a decrease in depressive symptoms and a surprising lift in personal well-being (Caputo, 2021). Freedom doesn't mean failure. It means you both get to thrive in your own ways.

## Space to Reimagine, Reclaim, and Rebuild

That space, once filled with others' needs, is now sacred. It's yours. For many women in midlife, it's the first time in decades that they get to ask themselves: What do *I* want? You may find yourself unsure how to answer. That's okay. We get rusty when we haven't practiced self-prioritization. We forget what it's like to wake up without being needed, or to spend a weekend doing something purely because it brings us joy, and not because it serves the family.

In fact, a 2023 study found that when midlife women began participating in social activities after their children left home (clubs, volunteering, or simply deeper friendships), their mental and physical health improved significantly (Wang et al., 2023). That sacred space can become a greenhouse for your personal bloom.

I remember looking around our home one day, while we were deep in the planning stages for the big move. I realized that every design decision, every storage bin, every cabinet was chosen for someone else's convenience. Now that they were grown and gone, I had the chance to restyle everything for *us*. This was not in a self-absorbed way, but in a self-honoring way. Today, after working with and helping so many other midlife folks make their own home transitions, I understand that this is the stage where many of us make one critical decision. We either decide to redesign our home life to better fit ourselves as we are now, or we allow it to remain frozen in time, memorializing a version of ourselves that no longer exists. Whichever option we choose can have big implications on how to treat every other aspect of our midlife journey and beyond.

## Redefining "Home" in the Absence of Mothering

The physical space you live in often reflects the emotional space you occupy. When the kids are gone, you might feel like you're walking through a home built for someone else's life. That's your invitation. You can start over, room by room if needed. There are no rules on how you do this, but it has to be a conscious move toward your next phase. You get to decide how you proceed and what areas you will focus on first.

Let the empty nest be a blank canvas, not a void. This might mean redecorating, repurposing rooms, or letting go of things you kept "just in case." But it also means updating the mental real estate. It's time to evict guilt, obligation, and martyrdom. Instead, you will move in joy, rest, curiosity, and desire.

## You Don't Need Permission to Prioritize Yourself

This is the part where you get to be a little selfish, finally. This is where you book the solo trip, start the new career, go back to school, rest more, date again, or just sit still long enough to hear yourself think. I want you to hear this message loud and clear. Midlife isn't the end of the road. It's a turnoff to a different highway. What's beautiful is you get to choose where it leads now. You are the main person you need to check in with as you get this journey started.

## So what does rediscovery actually look like?

It doesn't begin with a bucket list. It begins with a whisper. A whisper that might say, *"I miss me"*.

You may not have said those exact words, but maybe you've felt them in your body. It's in the slow mornings that no longer start with school drop-offs. It might be in the absence of chaos that once defined your day. Maybe it shows up in the grocery store, when you pause in front of a shelf and realize you don't even know what *you* like to eat anymore, because for the last two decades, someone else's preferences always came first. Don't get me started on how quickly my grocery bill changed after we became empty nesters. What used to look like a preschool snack time closet now looks like the pantry of people who have been on vacation for a few weeks. Daily cooking of full family meals is no longer a part of my grind.

There is a quiet ache in that realization, but also a powerful opportunity. That ache is the invitation to rediscover and reprioritize what you want. Ask yourself what *you* want when you choose a new place to go out for dinner. Think about what show *you* have been wanting to see. If the best time to go is on a random "school night", then even better. You're not getting up and operating the mom taxi anymore, so go out and indulge, even if it's a random weeknight.

In this next chapter of life, self-care isn't a luxury. It's a necessity. It is how we anchor ourselves to who we are becoming, not just who we've been for everyone else. It needs to be locked in on your daily to-do list as if your well being depends on it. Make it part of your hygiene routine. Lock it into your schedule and protect that time with intention. I'm not talking about the commercial self-care images that might come to mind. So much of that is likely just ways capitalist consumerism encourages us to buy more candles, and convinces us that overpriced skin care products are worth our pennies.

I'm referring to saying no to things you don't want to do and protecting your time. Maybe it is how you decide you will no longer take work home, or spend your weekends stressing over an inbox that never seems to clear. How about when you stop answering work emails and text messages after a certain hour in the evenings? Maybe you say "no" when you are asked to do something you have zero interest in, and you don't over-explain why. When you learn to stop explaining yourself to people who have not earned a spot on your priority list, that is a true victory.

Here's the sobering truth. We don't have forever. We're not old, but we're certainly not twenty. We have more years behind us than ahead of us, and while that might sting to acknowledge, it's not meant to be morbid. It's meant to be motivating. Because if not now…

when? The sooner you start intentionally creating space for your own joy, the sooner you can experience it.

## Choosing Yourself, On Purpose

I want you to imagine this next season of your life as a home that's being remodeled. The foundation is still strong. You've built it with love and sweat and sacrifice. But some of the rooms? They need updating. They were designed for someone else's comfort. Someone else's needs. There might be a nursery or a playroom. The garage is full of storage bins holding memories you're scared to let go of. That was the life you built for *them.* But now? Now, it's time to renovate for you. Think of your self-care as the first hammer swing.

Dr. Marcy Strahan is a respected self-care expert. She fiercely reminds us that self-care doesn't have to cost hundreds of dollars or happen in a luxury hotel. It can be as simple as deciding to put your own name on your list. When she does her famous exercise, of asking people to name the ten most important people in their lives, almost no one includes themselves. At least they don't at first. Even now, as you are reading this, you might struggle to add your own name to your mental list.

My dear, that ends today. If you don't get any other revelation out of reading this book, I at least wish for you to begin taking your midlife self-discovery seriously. In the beautifully direct words of Mel Robbins, "no one is coming" to do this for you. No one is going to tap you on the shoulder and grant you permission to go in search of your own joy. You're not selfish for wanting more or pursuing something different from what you've always had. You have outgrown certain phases of your life. Heck, I used to wear a size 4 (and was damn cute, too). But I don't anymore, so there is absolutely no reason for me to shop those sizes when I buy new clothes. I have literally outgrown that size, so there was a need to start looking for styles and fits that complement what I look like now.

The possibilities were wide open,, and I got to make all the choices without considering anyone else's needs. Maybe I will get back to that size 4 one day, or maybe I won't. What I do know is that if I do, I surely won't be interested in the outfits I liked when I was that age. I will be dressing as a mature, confident woman over 50, who prioritizes a different style and level of comfort. The same goes for you, as you look out onto the blank canvas of this new season of life. It is wide open with possibilities. You get to design it, one tiny decision at a time.

If you are still struggling with this idea of putting yourself first, I want you to remember this. You're not neglecting anyone by tending to your own needs. If you were setting out for a road trip, you would first need to fill up your gas tank for the journey. You map out the path to get where you're going, and maybe grab some food items to snack on and stay nourished. Think of prioritizing your self-care as a way of preparing for midlife, so you are proactively prepared for the journey. The more you regularly fill up your tank, the longer you will be able to go without issues. If you fail to do the prep work, then the journey will be difficult, plain and simple.

Repeat these words to yourself again and again: You're not too old to start dreaming again. You are simply remembering that you matter, too.

## Designing a Life You Don't Need to Escape From

The truth is, we have to stop thinking someone is coming to rescue us. Our kids don't need us in the same way. The roles we once played (mom, teacher, wife, caregiver, fixer) don't carry the same weight they once did. Besides, your worth is not attached to those roles. This is where you get to write a new script.

Jenet Dove, an innovative psychotherapist who works with women to overcome their perfectionist tendencies, shared how this and over-functioning often leave us emotionally malnourished. We've learned to hustle for our worth, to earn approval by being everything to everyone. But midlife invites us to question whether the life we've been living still fits, or if it ever really did. Let that sit for a minute.

For many of us, the answer is no. That is not failure. That's clarity. This is the moment to be brave enough to say, "I want something more", and selfish enough to pursue it without guilt. If you are still waiting for someone to give you permission to put yourself first, then here it is. You are allowed to step into this season of life with the intention of doing what brings you joy and fulfillment above all else. It doesn't have to be a public declaration you make out loud to anyone else. As long as you are clear about where your boundaries are and have a clear understanding of what feels right for you, the rest of us will receive the message just fine. Don't over-explain yourself. Don't apologize for saying no. Just start taking small steps in the direction of your future self. She is watching and eagerly waiting.

## Rest Is a Revolution

Let's be really honest. We've worn the "strong Black woman" badge like it was stitched to our DNA. It hasn't always been our fault, because generations have passed down this unspoken expectation. We got stuff done because we were often the most talented, educated, and innovative in any space. We know how to push through, hold it together, and make it happen. It was never celebrated because it was considered our baseline, and we never disputed it. We just continued to do what we do.

But now? Now we get to put that superwoman cape down. To be deeply revealing, the strong Black woman label only benefited everyone else, but never did a damn thing for us. Whenever I hear someone use this term, it feels like a backhanded compliment to be honest. It's as if they are really saying "thanks for showing up, doing all the grunt work no one else can do or be bothered with, so we look to you to get it done and not ask for anything in return, including proper credit or acknowledgement". Where is the lie?

Self-care, at this stage, is no longer optional. It's how we preserve the version of ourselves we haven't even met yet. Have you checked in on your blood pressure lately? What does your quality of sleep look like right now? When was the last time you had a full "me" day?

As a midlifer, rest might look like blocking your calendar for stillness. Or it might look like building a sanctuary corner in your home that belongs only to you. Maybe your rest means walking outside every evening because the sound of birds reminds you that you're still here.

Sometimes, it looks like saying "no", without explanation and without apology. Practice saying these phrases. No, I won't be attending that party. No, I won't volunteer this time. No, I don't want to carry that load anymore. Say each one out loud and then stop talking. Don't follow up by sharing more details as to why you are saying no.

There is oxygen on the other side of "no." There is freedom. Peace. Time.

## A Final Word: Time Is the Currency of Midlife

You spent years giving to everyone else. You were their calendar, their caretaker, their chef, their counselor, their safe place.

Now it's your turn to give to yourself. The kids may be grown… but *you're not done yet*. Sis, hear me when I say this: we don't have time to waste performing a version of ourselves that no longer fits. We can't keep saying "someday," "maybe later," and "after I take care of everything else." We've done that for years, or actually decades.

Now it's your time to breathe and dream. Take a little time to explore the woman underneath the layers of roles and responsibility. Get still enough to hear your own voice, and trust what it says.

This is the transition to rediscover the person underneath the role. Be intentional with letting joy come back in and stay for a while. The calendar is lighter. Then you might hear your soul whispering: "What about me?". Answer her, but not with guilt. Answer with joy and softness. Linger in a room of your own and mornings that move at your pace. Create a schedule that includes your name. Remember that tomorrow is not promised. But today? Today is yours.

### Reflection + Journaling Exercise: It's Your Turn Now

**Take your time with this. This isn't a test. It's a check-in — with yourself.**

Grab a quiet corner, your favorite pen, and a journal that feels worthy of your story. These prompts are here to help you peel back the layers of responsibility, old expectations, and outdated roles so you can meet the woman you are now — and the one you're becoming.

### 1. What have I been putting off because I felt I needed permission?

So many of us have dreams sitting on the shelf, gathering dust. We tell ourselves we'll get to them "once things calm down," or "once the kids are settled," or "once I retire." The truth is, we've been waiting for permission — often from people who aren't even paying attention.

What have you wanted to do that you haven't allowed yourself to begin?

Start the business? Join a dance class? Write a book? Redecorate your home? Sit in silence and *not* feel bad about it?

Write it all down, uncensored.

Then underline the one that makes your heart beat a little faster.

*"I've been putting off _____ because I thought I needed permission. But I don't. Not anymore."*

## 2. When was the last time I felt true joy, just for me?

Think back. Not to a moment where you were happy *because* your child succeeded or *because* everything was running smoothly. But a moment that lit *you* up from the inside. Maybe it was when you danced in the kitchen with no music. Maybe it was sitting on a beach alone. Maybe it was starting — and finishing — a puzzle, a book, or a project just because it delighted you.

Describe the moment in detail.

Where were you? What were you doing? What were you wearing, smelling, eating, or listening to?

More importantly, How can you recreate that feeling in your current life?

*"Joy felt like _____. I want more of that."*

## 3. What does my body need more of right now?

Your body has carried you through everything. Through pregnancies, surgeries, long workdays, sleepless nights, and endless caretaking. She's been there — often without thanks. Now, it's time to listen.

Does she need rest?

More movement?

A slower morning?

A bedtime routine that includes something other than scrolling your phone?

Less caffeine, more water?

Permission to stretch instead of sprint?

Write her a thank-you note. Then ask her what she needs — and promise to give her at least *one* thing this week.

*"This week, I will honor my body by _____."*

## 4. What do I want the next 5 years to feel like?

Notice we didn't say, *What do you want to accomplish.*

This isn't about a checklist, a promotion, or a dollar amount. This is about feeling.

Do you want your life to feel spacious? Quiet? Adventurous? Luxurious? Creative? Deeply peaceful?

Describe a typical day in that future life. What time do you wake up? What's the first thing you hear? What do you *not* do anymore? What do you say yes to?

Then ask yourself: What small step could I take this month to start living into that feeling now?

*"In the next season of my life, I want to feel _____. Today, I will take one step toward that by _____."*

## 5. What do I need to release in order to reclaim myself?

Let's call it out.

Is it guilt for taking up space?

Shame around aging?

The need to constantly prove your worth through productivity?

The role you played so well that you forgot it wasn't the whole story?

There are people, places, beliefs, and behaviors you may need to grieve and release. Not because they were bad, but because they've run their course.

And in their place? You get to plant something new.

Write a release statement that speaks directly to your spirit. You can whisper it, shout it, tape it to your mirror, or burn it in a candle ceremony if that feels good to you.

*"I release _____. I reclaim _____. I am not starting over. I'm starting deeper."*

# CHAPTER 11

## Less Stuff, More Self: Living lighter so you can feel more of what matters

At some point in midlife, your ambition shifts. You no longer crave "more" in the way you once did. We're talking about more clothes, more storage, or more things to prove. They just don't hit the same.

Instead, you start craving peace. You look for breathing room. Simplicity becomes a priority because who's got time for all that? What you really feel is that you don't want to spend energy on things that no longer make you feel good. You don't want to fill your space. You want your space to serve you. You want a home and a life that feels like a soft exhale instead of another to-do list.

I remember when my husband and I purchased our first home. We put on a big wedding, but chose to forego spending money on a honeymoon. The larger goal was throwing every dollar toward our new house. After being a couple for four years and managing two separate apartments during that phase of our relationship, you might think combining our households would be a lot.

But it was just the two of us back then. Outside of the primary bedroom, living room, and main bathroom, most of the other spaces of the new house sat empty. As a newlywed eager to make our home feel warm and inviting, I shopped at every big box home décor store in town. My cart overflowed with mass-produced wall art, colorful throw pillows, and countless trinkets that served no purpose other than filling up space. Don't get me wrong. It worked. Every home we've had over the years has been cozy, welcoming, and ready to host for the holidays and other celebrations.

Those early days were wonderful, no doubt. I have so much gratitude for the disciplined mindset we held back then. I loved how that first purchase made our families proud and created a home base where we could all gather for our annual Thanksgiving feast.

As young professionals from humble beginnings, we would've gladly sacrificed our most prized possessions for just one glimpse of that look of pride on our parents' faces. We're talking about giving up our *Boyz II Men* and *TLC* CDs, and even that '90s era silk shirt we wore to every grown folks' function. We would've handed over our last pair of bamboo earrings, boxed up our *New Edition* posters, and kissed our carefully curated mixtapes goodbye (yes, even the one with *Illmatic* on one side and *My Life* on the other). That's because in that moment, nothing mattered more than making our parents proud.

With all our Gen X peers, we weren't just working for ourselves. We were carrying the dreams of the generations before us. We're only one degree removed from segregation and the Civil Rights Movement. Our parents and grandparents didn't just live through struggle. They survived it with grit, prayer, and a deep belief that life could be better for their children.

Buying a home in a beautiful suburb wasn't just a real estate goal. It was a full-circle moment. It was proof that the sacrifice wasn't in vain. That all the marching, scrimping, saving, and saying "yes" to jobs they hated were worth it. This is because we were the ones who finally got to sign the deed, paint the nursery, and grill in the backyard without fear or limitation.

So, of course, we held onto that dream tight. Of course, we bought all the furniture, filled the cabinets, and made sure the holiday décor changed with the seasons. We weren't just decorating. We were honoring a legacy.

But now that we're older, wiser, and feeling the weight of maintaining it all, a new question begins to rise. *Is this still the dream I want?* Or is it time to dream something different? Maybe we need something that feels lighter, freer, and rooted in who I've become, not just where I came from.

## Redefining the Dream in Midlife

The dreams we were raised with were sacred, but that doesn't mean they have to be permanent.

Midlife is the perfect season to pause and ask: *What do I actually want now?* It's not necessarily  what my parents wanted for me. It might not be what society told me was the definition of success. Or maybe it's not what looked good in a family Christmas card. What do I, with my full-grown wisdom and slightly creaky knees, want from the life I still have left to live?

Maybe you're realizing that owning a big home isn't the flex it used to be. Maybe the silence of an empty nest is calling you to something quieter, simpler, or more soulful. Maybe you're finally willing to say out loud that you don't want to maintain the yard, clean all those extra rooms, or keep paying for a storage unit full of "just in case" furniture.

I want to drive this point home: shifting your dream doesn't mean you're ungrateful. It means you're evolving. It means you've given yourself permission to prioritize joy over obligation. Ease over status. Presence over performance.

Redefining the dream in midlife might look like:

- Renting an apartment with a walkable lifestyle so you can explore new restaurants, theaters, and weekend farmers' markets.

- Traveling more, even if that means trading a mortgage for a passport.

- Spending less time managing stuff and more time nurturing relationships that fill your cup.

- Downsizing your home so you can upsize your peace.

This isn't about giving up. It's about shifting the spotlight from what you've achieved to how you actually want to feel every day. Sometimes, the most revolutionary thing you can do is give yourself permission to want something else.

## Your Stuff Is a Mirror

Your belongings are not neutral. They're reflections of your identity, aspirations, fears, or obligations. That jacket in the back of your closet? It still has the tags on it because it represents a version of you that others expected, rather than who you truly are. What about that crystal punch bowl gathering dust in your overflowing china cabinet? It symbolizes a societal ideal of being the perfect hostess, even if your soul thrives in intimate dinners or quiet evenings alone.

The extra dishes in your cabinets represent not preparedness but fear of inadequacy, the "what if" of not measuring up when guests arrive. These items weigh heavier than their physical presence suggests. They anchor you to insecurities and outdated dreams.

Research from Princeton University shows that clutter can actually inhibit your brain's ability to process information effectively (McMains, S., & Kastner, S., 2011). Clutter doesn't just occupy physical space; it consumes mental space, leaving you fatigued, anxious, and overwhelmed.

## The Weight of "Just in Case"

"Just in case" is a common phrase among midlifers, representing the reluctance to fully embrace change:

- Just in case the kids move back.

- Just in case I lose weight.

- Just in case I finally throw that party.

- Just in case life reverts to how it used to be.

Holding onto these "just in case" items prevents you from fully inhabiting your present. It keeps you tethered to hypothetical futures or past versions of yourself, creating an ongoing emotional strain.

Psychologists at UCLA found that excessive clutter can elevate cortisol, your stress hormone, negatively impacting both physical and mental health (Saxbe, D. E., Repetti, R., 2010). Letting go isn't just about creating space. It's a vital act of your self-care.

## Living With Less Doesn't Mean Settling

Choosing simplicity isn't about deprivation. It's about intentionality. Minimalism isn't solely about aesthetics. It's a mindset shift that empowers you to ask: *Do my surroundings reflect who I truly am and who I aspire to become?*

Studies from the University of California show that people who prioritize experiences over possessions experience greater happiness and fulfillment (Gilovich, T., Kumar, A., & Jampol, L., 2015). Aligning your environment with your values creates a richer life, filled with meaning rather than stuff.

Living lighter can be luxurious. I am not at all advocating that you start living like you're taking a vow of poverty. Honey, it's just the opposite. You should be able to splurge on beautiful things or experiences in your midlife season. The difference is that you can be more mindful about where you direct those hard-earned dollars. When you stop throwing money at things that no longer serve you, you can redirect those funds to what you really do want.

One simple a-ha moment I had was at the nail salon of all places. Sis, you know what I am talking about. It was that part of the visit when the nail technician tries to upsell you on the premium service, when all you came in for was a quick touch-up. By default, I was so used to saying "no thank you" because the price of that one service was higher than I felt it was worth. However, this time I took time to do some fast math. I realized that if the premium service truly lasted longer and I would not have to come back for another month, then it would cost less than my bi-weekly routine in the long run. I agreed to the higher-priced service, and yes, the treatment did work like he promised. Overall, my money and my time were saved.

The idea stuck with me. What other spending habits was I holding on to that were costing me more money? This wholesale shopping mentality I'd adopted over the years was causing me to purchase higher quantities of cheaper, lower lower-quality products, all of which I would burn through quickly. When the quality was substandard, they simply would not last. The buy-one-get-one cheap t-shirts would not make it through more than a couple of wash cycles. The knock-off leather handbag would start peeling, or the seams would unravel. When I have been more mindful about purchasing higher-quality products, I have really saved money in the long run because I wasn't having to replace those items too quickly.

Something else I stopped doing in recent years was buying a lot of presents, especially during the holidays. Now, before you start clutching your pearls in shock, let me explain. My young nieces and nephews are exempt from this rule, by the way. They most definitely are on my gift-buying list. But for grown working adults, it is a little different. I still love to celebrate loved ones on their special days, but now I opt to splurge on them with experiences and prioritize time together. I am the friend who will make a reservation for dinner at a beautiful restaurant where we can enjoy each other's company and just be pampered for the evening. Maybe I'll surprise you with concert tickets or a night out to an NBA game. My gift is to spoil you for a little while. I am not the friend who will scour the stores, looking for a random gift item to give you, which might not be something you would want for yourself anyway. My gamble is that you will remember and appreciate the experiences we shared together more.

If spoiling your loved ones with material gifts makes you feel good, don't let my personal philosophy change your mind. The point is you get to do you in this season. You don't have to please anyone else in order to please yourself. You might not be rich in material wealth (yet), but you could be, in how rich your life feels when it isn't weighed down by clutter, chaos, or unmet expectations.

## Releasing the Version of You That Accumulated It All

We accumulate "stuff" during survival years, by raising kids, building careers, caring for others, and keeping the wheels turning. During that time, our homes become warehouses of convenience and comfort.

Midlife gives us a rare opportunity: to acknowledge the strength it took to survive those years and to ask boldly: *What do I want next?* Decluttering isn't just about the objects. It's about honoring who you were and making room for who you're becoming.

## More Room to Feel, Dream, and Just Be

After my own decluttering journey, weekends transformed from exhausting cleaning marathons to spontaneous adventures. Financial resources once tied up in maintaining clutter became investments in experiences and relationships that nourished my soul. Simplicity didn't restrict my life. It liberated it.

The magic of "less" is that it leaves room for more of what actually matters:

More time.

More clarity.

More ease.

More authenticity.

And most importantly, more you.

## Minimalism for Beginners: A Practical Approach

During this time, I started to learn more about the concept of minimalism. Minimalism isn't about stark white walls or owning fewer than ten items. It's about intentional living. Minimalism isn't about having bare walls, white furniture, or living out of a suitcase with only 30 items. That's one version, but it's not the only one. At its core, minimalism is about making space for what truly matters by clearing out what doesn't. It's the practice of being intentional about the things you bring into your life... your home, your schedule, your relationships, your spending.

It's asking yourself these questions. Does this still serve me? Does this bring me peace or joy? Or is it just taking up space and energy?

For midlifers especially, minimalism is less about aesthetics and more about freedom. It's about releasing the weight of things we've been holding on to, physically and emotionally. You have held on to them out of guilt, fear, or habit. It's about designing a life that feels light, aligned, and rooted in the now.

You don't need to throw everything away or live in an empty apartment to be a minimalist. You just need to begin choosing more consciously what you want to carry forward with you, and what you're finally ready to let go of.

Here are basic steps to start your journey:

1. **Assess** – Go room-by-room, drawer-by-drawer, asking, "Does this item serve me now?"

2. **Categorize** – Use the four-box method: Keep, Donate, Sell, Trash.

3. **One-Year Rule** – If you haven't used or thought about it in over a year, let it go.

4.  **Mindful Purchasing** – Before buying something new, pause. Will this truly serve your life as it is today?

## Let It Sink In

If reading this stirred something in you, like a memory, a truth you've been avoiding, or even a little twinge of guilt, then you're not alone. Let it wash over you. This part of the journey isn't about judgment; it's about clarity.

Listen, we've all kept a throw pillow or three that no one's allowed to sit on, saved a rice cooker we forgot we owned, or held onto jeans that haven't zipped up since the Clinton administration. You're in good company.

The truth is, many of us have been living out dreams handed to us with love and good intentions. But just because your mama fought for a four-bedroom house with a formal living room doesn't mean you're obligated to dust that furniture forever. It's okay to change your mind. It's okay to want something lighter, quieter, and more you.

You've spent decades building, nurturing, striving, and sustaining. Now, you've earned the right to ask: What do I want this next season to feel like? Let's slow it down and turn the lens inward. No, not to tear anything down, but to finally make space for what's been waiting patiently in the wings: your desires, your voice, your vision.

What follows isn't homework. It's a homecoming. This is your permission slip to get honest with yourself, and maybe to finally toss that bread maker you've never used. You know the one.

Take your time. Be real. Most of all, be kind to yourself.

**Reflection: Redesigning Your Dream**

Take a deep breath. This is your space to dream, not the version you were handed, but the version that feels aligned with who you are now. Grab a journal, a quiet moment, and answer honestly:

1. What parts of the dream I inherited still feel good to me today?

2. What parts of that dream feel like they belong to someone else, or a former version of me?

3. If I could design my life from scratch today, what would I want more of? Less of?

4. What am I willing to release to make room for what I truly want?

5. How will I know I'm living my redefined dream? What will it look like, sound like, and feel like in my body?

**Bonus Invitation:** Write a vision letter to your future self, 5 years from now. Describe what your day looks like in this redefined life, like where you live, how you feel, who you spend time with, and how you've created a space and lifestyle that finally reflects you.

# PART THREE

## SELF

# CHAPTER 12

## Nah, That's a Boundary: Redefining Your Limits and Protecting Your Peace Without Apology

There comes a moment in midlife when you stop bending to make others comfortable and finally start standing in your own truth. That moment doesn't arrive with confetti. It usually shows up quietly, after years of emotional exhaustion, after a burnout you couldn't quite name, and after one too many times of putting yourself last on your own list.

For decades, many of us wore overcommitment like a badge of honor. We said yes on autopilot. We said yes to overtime, yes to last-minute requests, yes to other people's drama and dysfunction, and yes to expectations we never even agreed to. In the process, we shrank ourselves to make room for everyone else's comfort and chaos. That became our normal. That became our survival. We made it look easy, even as it silently drained the life out of us.

A recent research study explored why we do this. This study explores "John Henryism," a term used to describe the high-effort coping style where Black individuals push themselves relentlessly to overcome adversity. This behavior is common in midlife Black women, particularly professionals. The study found that this constant pushing leads to worse self-rated health unless individuals balance it with protective strategies like rest and boundary-setting (Robinson et al., 2022).

One lesson life has taught me is this: your "yes" loses its value when you never use your "no". Rewind and look at that statement again. Midlife is the season where your voice gets stronger, clearer, and more aligned with your values. You stop asking for permission to protect your peace. You stop explaining why you're no longer available for environments that deplete you. You stop performing for approval and start practicing boundaries rooted in self-respect.

Setting boundaries is not about pushing others away. It is about staying anchored in what matters to you. Boundaries keep you centered. They are what protect the version of yourself you are working so hard to become. Without boundaries, burnout becomes the norm. With them, balance becomes possible. The difference between those two realities comes down to one decision: whether you choose yourself.

Let's get one thing straight right now. Saying "nah" does not make you mean. It makes you clear. It means you've stopped sacrificing your well-being on the altar of someone else's comfort. It means you've stopped apologizing for needing time, rest, or space. It means you've given yourself permission to live on your terms without waiting for someone else to co-sign.

Not everyone will be happy about your new boundaries. Some people will call you selfish, distant, or different. Let them. Their discomfort is not your responsibility to manage. Your job is not to explain your evolution to people who benefited from your lack of boundaries. Your job is to manage your energy like it's your most valuable asset. You get one body, one mind, and one life. Boundaries are how you protect that gift.

The more you practice saying no, the easier it gets. What once felt confrontational will start to feel like clarity. What used to give you anxiety will begin to give you peace. You'll stop overexplaining. You'll stop negotiating. You'll stop raising your hand for chaos. You'll learn to say, "nah," and mean it from your core.

If you're worried it's too late to start enforcing boundaries, I'm here to tell you that midlife is the best reason to start. This is your checkpoint. You've given enough and performed enough. Now is the time to reclaim your joy and peace without guilt or apology. You're allowed to leave the group chat. You're allowed to change your mind. You're allowed to sit things out. You're allowed to walk away from people who drain you, even if they share your DNA. You're allowed to be unavailable.

The version of you who always kept the peace might not survive this season, and that's okay. She did her job. Let her rest. Let her be proud that you finally stepped up and took the baton. Now it's your turn to run this leg of the race, but with boundaries, with joy, and with full permission to choose yourself first.

So how do you actually begin? How do you move from being the go-to person for everyone else to becoming the one who fiercely protects your own time, energy, and well-being? You start with the truth: that you have nothing left to prove. You do not have to wear exhaustion as evidence of your worth. You do not have to earn rest. You are allowed to be whole, even if that means disappointing some people along the way. Let me tell you how I finally learned that lesson.

**Protecting your peace is not optional. It's sacred. It starts with a simple, holy word: "Nah."**

There was a time when the idea of disappointing my colleagues would send me into a spiral. The younger, less secure version of me was addicted to being liked. I'm not talking about casual approval. I mean, it was the full-on dopamine hit that came from being the dependable one, the fixer, the one who could handle anything with a smile. I stayed late, took on extra projects, volunteered for the tasks no one wanted, and made it all look effortless. Deep down, I was convinced that being seen as exceptional would shield me from criticism, invisibility, or being passed over.

Over time, I learned that being liked is not the same as being respected. Constantly playing superwoman didn't make me feel safer. It just made me tired. The more mature, wiser version of me knows now that I can do excellent work, lead with integrity, and support my team without depleting myself. My value doesn't increase every time I say yes when my plate is already full. I no longer equate over-functioning with job security. I have nothing to prove by overextending myself, and I no longer need external validation to confirm what I already know. I'm more than enough just as I am.

Let's go ahead and get something straight right out the gate: Saying no is not rude. Saying no is not mean. Saying no is not a character flaw. Saying no is an act of self-preservation. It's a declaration that you are no longer in the business of bleeding yourself dry to keep everyone else comfortable. That might sound harsh to some, but for us, Black women in midlife who have been the backbone, the default, the fixer, and the go-to for everybody and their mama, this is a lifeline.

From the time we were little girls, we were conditioned to be helpful, humble, polite, and strong. Oh, and we were strong above all else. Strong when it hurts. Strong when we were tired. Strong when we needed help but didn't feel safe asking. That "Strong Black Woman" trope became a trap. One that told us we are only valuable when we are doing the most. It's the one that convinced us we had to earn rest. One that applauded our ability to hold everything and everyone together, while no one checked if we were okay.

Let me go ahead and say it: You are allowed to put the cape down. You've worn it long enough. If we're being honest, it's heavy. It's suffocating. It's keeping you stuck in cycles of burnout, resentment, and invisibility. Sis, you deserve more.

I didn't always know this. There was a time when I measured my worth by how much I could take on. At work, I was the dependable one. The yes-woman. The one who could juggle it all and still show up to the 8 a.m. Zoom call camera-ready. At home, I was the caregiver, the planner, the emotional support system for everybody in my orbit. I had convinced myself that saying yes made me valuable. That being everything for everyone was noble. Then one day, I found myself crying in my parked car, not from sadness, but from soul-level exhaustion. I had nothing left to give, and worse, I didn't even know how to ask for what I needed.

That day, I gave myself permission to start practicing a new kind of strength. The kind that says, "No, I can't do that." The kind that says, "Actually, I need a minute." The kind that makes peace a priority instead of a maybe. Saying no wasn't easy at first. It felt like betrayal, of other people's expectations and the version of myself I had spent years building. Yet every 'no' I spoke aloud became a little more liberating. It felt a little more truthful. It was a little more like coming home to myself.

One of the most powerful moments came on a Friday afternoon when a colleague sent me a last-minute request for a deliverable. My old self would've canceled dinner plans, opened the laptop, and gotten it done, no questions asked. This time, I replied with a simple: "Unfortunately, I won't be able to take this on." I didn't offer a long-winded explanation. I didn't fumble through a fake apology. I just delivered a clear, firm sentence. Here's what happened: nothing. The world kept turning. I wasn't fired. The project got reassigned. What I received was even better… an evening of my own. I went for a walk. I ate dinner without multitasking. I took a deep breath and felt peace settle into my bones.

That's when it clicked. You don't have to earn rest. You don't have to explain your no. You don't have to be everything to everyone.

Here's my hot take: I no longer believe it's my employer's job to protect my work-life balance. That's on me. It took years to realize that nobody was coming to rescue me from burnout. I had to put myself at the top of my own priority list. That doesn't mean I accept being overworked or mistreated. It means I take full ownership of how I show up. I've learned to be strategic, efficient, and protective of my time. I automate repetitive daily tasks. I create systems that work for me. I pay attention to my energy and schedule my deep focus work during my peak hours. When the workday ends, I log off. I don't check my email at midnight or squeeze in "just one more thing" out of guilt. I don't need a badge of honor for always being available. That mindset almost took me out. As a small business owner, I know there are seasons when the hustle is real and the grind is necessary. I'm not allergic to hard work and compete at an elite level when necessary. What I've outgrown is being in a constant state of self-neglect. There are also seasons when I can close the laptop, put the superwoman cape down, and breathe without apologizing for it. That is balance. That is grown woman energy. I stopped waiting for permission to protect my peace and started building my life around it.

If you're being honest, how much of your exhaustion is coming from the work itself, and how much is coming from the *way* you work? That is not always an easy question to face. For years, many of us wore our productivity like armor. We responded to emails before sunrise and stayed online long after the workday should have ended. We convinced ourselves that being accessible at all times meant we were committed, valuable, and irreplaceable. We said yes to every ask, even when our plates were already full. That's because we did not want to be seen as unavailable or disengaged. Somewhere along the way, the boundary between work and life disappeared, and we just kept pushing forward.

Midlife offers a chance to revisit all of that. You have the wisdom now to realize that nonstop hustle without pause is not a badge of honor. It is a self-destructive recipe. You can be excellent at your job and still protect your peace. You can deliver results and still draw a hard line when the workday ends. You can be a leader and still turn your notifications off after hours. This season of your life is calling you to be more intentional with your time and energy.

Start by observing your own patterns. Notice whether you're checking your email constantly out of reflex or anxiety, and not necessity. Pay attention to how often you accept meetings that do not need to happen, or say yes to projects that do not align with your role or capacity. Ask yourself if you are skipping lunch, staying late, or taking work home, not because it's truly required, but because you are still stuck in that old mindset of having to prove yourself. Sometimes we carry over habits that are no longer useful, simply because they used to serve a version of us that no longer exists.

This is your moment to shift. Maybe that looks like setting a true end time to your workday and sticking to it, even when you feel the urge to "just finish one more thing." Maybe it means blocking time on your calendar for actual focused work so your entire day isn't swallowed up by back-to-back meetings. Maybe it means taking your lunch away from your desk. Maybe it means giving yourself permission to move slower, to breathe, to stop operating like your worth is directly tied to your productivity.

There will always be seasons that require extra energy. If you run a business or lead a team, you know there are times when the demands are high and the deadlines are real. You will rise to the occasion. You always do. The difference now is that when those seasons pass, you will no longer default to staying in overdrive. Those are opportune times to throttle back. You will know how to rest. You will trust that you do not have to live in crisis mode just to be seen as competent.

None of this is about perfection. It is about paying attention. It is about choosing what truly matters over what simply fills the calendar. It is about understanding that your rest is not a luxury. It is a right. You do not have to earn it. You simply have to honor it.

**Try This: Reclaim Your Workday**

Look at your calendar and schedule an intentional sign-off time for the end of your workday. Set a reminder if you need to. When the time arrives, power down your computer, silence your work notifications, and step away without guilt.

Audit your daily tasks. Ask yourself which activities truly move your goals forward and which ones feel performative. Where can you delegate? What can be automated? What can wait?

Choose one boundary you will protect this week. It could be a real lunch break, where you are not in front of screens. It could be not replying to emails after 6 p.m. It could be declining a meeting that does not need your presence. Start small and be consistent.

Take a moment to reflect on your work-life rhythm. No, not just your schedule, but also your patterns. Look at your tendencies and the way you move through the day. Are you still operating from the habits of a younger, over-proving version of yourself? The one who believed being exhausted meant you were successful? The one who raised her hand for every task, stayed late without boundaries, and thought saying "no" would make people question her worth?

If you recognize her, don't shame her. Thank her. She got you here.

That younger version of you did what she had to do. She figured it out without a blueprint. She played the game, kept the peace, and read every room before she spoke. She knew how to survive in systems that weren't built with her in mind. She found ways to thrive anyway. She took the risks. She swallowed her frustration. She endured countless microaggressions. She also made herself undeniable. She learned the hard lessons that paved the way for the ease with which you are allowed to choose now.

So what about now? You are not her anymore.

You have done the work. You have earned your voice, your wisdom, and your proverbial seat at the table. You no longer need to lead with exhaustion as proof of commitment. You no longer need to shape-shift just to stay in the room. You get to build a rhythm that honors the version of you that exists today, which is more grounded, more selective, and definitely more at peace.

This is the moment to look forward.

In a previous chapter, we explored the practice of imagining your future self, the one you are growing into. She is not running on fumes. She is not apologizing for needing space. She is not booked and busy just to prove she is valuable. She is focused, clear, and deliberate. She chooses rest with the same confidence she once chose hustle.

She is waiting for you to catch up to her.

So, as you reassess your workday, ask yourself: Am I still moving from survival mode, or am I moving in alignment with who I am becoming? Does my calendar reflect my values or just my obligations? Am I chasing approval, or am I walking in my purpose?

The truth is, your future self cannot meet you until you slow down long enough to recognize her.

You do not owe anyone access to every minute of your day. You do not need to stay in overdrive to be respected. You are allowed to move differently now.

Begin rewriting the rhythm. It won't happen all at once. It might not occur with a grand gesture. Start small. Start by noticing. Start by giving yourself permission to feel differently about how you work, when you rest, and what you say yes to. Then start building a schedule that honors the life you are creating, not the one you outgrew.

This is not about doing less just for the sake of slowing down. This is about doing what matters with more presence and more peace.

You have earned that right. Let the version of you who fought to get here rest for a while. The version of you who is still becoming is ready to take the lead.

**Boundaries allow for rest**

So many of us, especially those of us raised with big responsibilities on small shoulders, still think we need to check every box before we're allowed to sit down. We believe we must be tired enough, productive enough, or needed enough to justify taking a damn nap. Let me go ahead and shatter that myth right now: Rest is not a reward. It's your birthright.

You don't have to be productive to deserve peace. You don't have to be exhausted to earn sleep. You don't need anyone's permission to unplug. Resting doesn't make you lazy. It makes you wise.

Boundaries are the gatekeepers of that wisdom. They are not walls to keep people out. They are filters to protect what matters most. Boundaries keep you from saying yes when your spirit is screaming no. They protect your energy from emotional leeches who always call you for advice but are never around when you need support. They help you unplug from workplace guilt that tells you to always be available, even during your off hours. Boundaries are not selfish. They are sacred.

Now, let's be real. Some of y'all need boundaries with your own damn self. That includes not checking your work email at 10 PM just because you're anxious. Not agreeing to go to every social gathering simply because someone invited you. Not pretending you're "fine" when your body is begging you to slow down. Self-abandonment is still abandonment, even when you're the one doing it.

I had to learn how to stop betraying myself in the name of being nice, helpful, or reliable. I had to learn how to honor my own needs even when nobody else noticed or understood. Protecting my peace became *my* responsibility. It all started with saying no, without guilt.

Here's what happens when you finally start doing that. At first, you will feel uncomfortable. Saying no, especially to people you love, will feel foreign and selfish. You'll second-guess yourself. You'll worry about being seen as rude or difficult. Stay with it. On the other side of that discomfort is a life that feels like yours again.

Eventually, you'll notice the people who genuinely respect you won't be offended by your boundaries. They'll honor them. Those who don't? Their reaction will tell you everything you need to know. Boundaries will reveal who's truly in your corner and who's just comfortable with your compliance.

When you begin choosing yourself consistently, when you honor your limits, protect your time, and prioritize your joy, you will feel lighter. Not because life gets easier, but because you are no longer carrying everyone else's weight on your back. You are finally showing up for the most important person in your life: you.

Let me be crystal clear. Joy is a boundary, too. Joy is not a frivolous extra you sprinkle on top after you've done all the hard stuff. It is essential. It is medicine. It is resistance. In a world that would rather you stay tired, overworked, and overextended, choosing joy on purpose is a radical act.

Start protecting your joy the same way you protect your time. Make space for the things that make you feel alive, whether that's dancing to old-school Janet in your living room, taking a solo trip to the coast, painting, gardening, or reading something juicy with your phone on do-not-disturb. The most important part? You don't need a reason. You don't need to accomplish anything to deserve beauty. You don't have to grind before you give yourself grace.

Sis, protect your peace like it's your job. It truly is. You have done more than enough. You have served, supported, led, and sacrificed. This is your time now. The next chapter of your life does not need to revolve around overfunctioning for others. It can be rooted in delight. It can be shaped by softness. It can be anchored in sovereignty. It can be filled with joy.

So, the next time someone asks you to do something that feels like a no, say it with your whole chest. No apology is needed. No explanation has to be provided. Just: "Nah. That's a boundary." Then go take care of yourself.

Now, I want you to pause for a moment. Take a deep breath. Let all of that sink in. Everything you've just read was not meant to overwhelm you. It was meant to affirm what you already know deep down: that you are worthy of peace, worthy of joy, and worthy of protection.

This is not just theory. This is your life. And your life deserves to be lived with intention, not by default. You don't have to have it all figured out right now, but I want you to start listening to yourself more closely. The part of you that's been whispering, "This doesn't feel right." That's the part that's tired of over-functioning and under-feeling. It's the part that's ready for softness.

## REFLECTION: Honor Your Boundaries, Reclaim Your Joy

Take a quiet moment for yourself. Breathe deep. Light a candle. Sit somewhere that feels peaceful, or at least where no one is asking you to do something for them.

These questions are for you. This is not a performance. This is not a moment for wearing a mask. This is a moment for truth.

Write your answers in a journal, on your notes app, or speak them aloud if that's more your flow. The goal isn't to be profound. It's to be real.

## 1. Where in your life do you feel the most drained right now?

Start here. Don't gloss over it. What part of your life makes your body sigh with exhaustion when you think about it?

Is it your job, the way it consumes your evenings and weekends, even after you've clocked out?

Is it a one-sided friendship that always has you pouring but never being poured into?

Is it your role in the family as the default fixer, scheduler, caregiver, and emotional manager?

Name it. Be specific. You can't reclaim your energy if you don't first identify what's draining it.

Sometimes we get so used to carrying the load that we forget it's heavy. Pay attention to what leaves you feeling resentful or depleted after the fact. That's a boundary waiting to be built.

## 2. What do you keep saying yes to that should have been a no?

Think about the last few weeks.

What did you agree to out of guilt, fear, or obligation instead of joy or alignment?

Maybe it was volunteering at an event you had no time for.

Maybe it was picking up someone else's slack at work because "you're just so good at it."

Maybe it was entertaining a conversation, relationship, or commitment that your spirit has already outgrown.

Now ask yourself why you said yes. Were you afraid of disappointing someone? Worried about what they'd think of you? Chasing their approval more than your own peace?

The next time that situation comes up, you get to choose differently. You are not required to be available to everything that asks for you. Your yes should be sacred, not automatic.

## 3. What does rest look like for you? What does joy feel like for you?

We talk a lot about needing rest and wanting joy. But have you ever taken the time to define those things on your own terms?

What does real, nourishing rest look like in your life?

Is it sleeping in without guilt?

Is it having an unscheduled Saturday with nowhere to be and no one to answer to?

Is it turning your phone off for a few hours and not explaining why?

What about joy? What makes you light up without effort?

Think beyond big events. Is it a morning walk? Dancing in your kitchen to 90s R&B? Calling a friend who makes you laugh until your stomach hurts?

Your joy and your rest don't have to be grand or performative. They just have to be real. You are allowed to build your day around what feeds your soul, not what drains it.

## 4. What boundaries would you set if you weren't worried about disappointing anyone?

Now we're getting to the juicy part.

If people-pleasing weren't a factor, what would change in your life *today*?

Would you stop picking up the phone when certain people call?

Would you start leaving work on time and stop apologizing for it?

Would you tell your family, "I'm not cooking this year. I'm resting?"

Would you step back from a friendship, relationship, or group chat that no longer aligns?

Write it all down, even if it scares you. Especially if it scares you.

You don't have to do all of it at once. But naming the boundary is the first act of power. Most of us are not as trapped as we think. We're just terrified of what it means to choose ourselves publicly.

## 5. What is one boundary you can put in place this week that protects your time, energy, or mental health?

Start with something small and doable, but make sure it honors your truth.

Maybe it's setting a hard stop to your workday at 6 PM, no matter what.

Maybe it's saying no to an invite without an excuse or fake apology.

Maybe it's deciding not to engage in gossip or venting calls that leave you feeling worse.

Maybe it's choosing to rest instead of proving how productive you can be.

Pick just one.

Put it into action this week.

Say it aloud.

Write it down.

Tell someone you trust.

Then honor it like your future self is depending on you, because she is.

You are not selfish for choosing peace. You are not difficult for saying no. You are not broken because you need rest. You are not unloving for loving yourself first. Every boundary you draw is a step toward becoming the most whole, rested, and joyful version of yourself. That woman, the one you are becoming, is not burned out, overbooked, or bitter. She is clear. She is free. She is thriving.

So go ahead and say it with your chest: Nah. That's a boundary.

# CHAPTER 13

## If They Wanted To, They Would: Stop chasing people, titles, and approval that don't see your worth

Let's tell the uncomfortable truth about what it is like to be a professional of color in America. For far too long, we've been trained to make ourselves palatable, professional, pleasing, and predictable. We were told that if we just stayed humble, waited our turn, smiled more, and didn't cause too much trouble, the things we longed for would eventually arrive. Respect. Visibility. Opportunity. Love.

We learned how to shrink without being taught how to expand. We found ourselves code-switching so hard we forgot what our original voice even sounded like. We stayed in jobs where we were praised quietly but passed over loudly. We clung to friendships where we were the consistent giver, always the one to text first and plan the outings, and remember the birthdays. Somewhere along the way, we started to believe that crumbs were better than nothing.

Midlife has a funny way of waking you all the way up.

There comes a moment. Maybe it's while you're listening to Mary J. in traffic, or while scrolling through old photos trying to remember when you last felt like yourself. It's when you realize the chasing has to stop. You're too grown and too seasoned to be trying to convince folks of your worth. One of the most freeing revelations you can have is simple, profound, and kind of brutal: if they wanted to, they would.

If they wanted to call, they would have. If they wanted to show up, they would have. If they wanted to love you the way you need and not just the way they feel like giving, they would have.

When they don't, you let them. Let them do what they do. Let them drift. Let them ghost. Let them misunderstand you. Let them unfriend you in real life. Let them not be ready. That is no longer your assignment to fix.

This is not about bitterness. This is about clarity. Midlife teaches you how to tell the difference. The reset you are in right now is not just professional. It is deeply personal, too.

This chapter is not just about a job title you didn't get. It is about all the spaces you showed up for fully, hoping someone would meet you halfway. It is about the moments you found yourself sitting in a room, wondering why your effort never seemed to be reciprocated, whether in your career, your friendships, or your family. It is about every time you felt invisible, even while doing the absolute most.

You may not have had the words for it then, but you do now. You have crossed enough milestones to know who you are. You have survived enough heartbreak to understand your value. You have raised kids, buried loved ones, earned degrees, started over, shown up when it hurt, and still kept your grace. That deserves better than one-sided connections.

When you stop chasing, something beautiful happens. You start attracting.

Friendships in this grown folks season of life come with a different rhythm. In your twenties, staying connected was easy. You saw your people every day at work, at school, or at happy hour. Your whole crew could be rounded up with a single text or a quick stop at the mall. Life was light, spontaneous, and wide open. You had time.

You had proximity. The relationships maintained themselves because your environments kept you naturally close.

That is no longer the case. Your best friend might live across the country. Your favorite cousin may only be active in the group chat once every six months. Everyone is navigating their own shift. There is nothing wrong with the love. The method has just changed.

Long silences do not always mean the love has disappeared. Sometimes a quick meme says, "I'm thinking of you". Sometimes a two-minute voice memo hits deeper than a two-hour phone call. Sometimes a once-a-year catch-up feels like no time has passed at all. The bond is still there, just living in a different season.

This is where creativity comes in. You do not have to give up on the people you love. You just have to allow the connection to evolve. That monthly dinner may now be a quarterly meetup. That talk-every-day friend may now be a talk-when-it-matters friend. You get to redefine what consistency means. It may not look like it did in the 90s, when friendships were built on cassette tapes, landlines, and full-day hangouts. It can still be just as meaningful.

Even with all the grace and understanding, there are relationships that will not make the cut.

Not because either of you did something wrong, but because growth is not always mutual. You are no longer the same version of yourself that you were when some of those friendships were formed. You have changed. Your values have shifted. Your priorities have evolved. That means some connections that once felt like home now feel like a costume.

We do not talk enough about how hard it is to release people you once built your life around. The friend who knew your pager code. The one who took the Greyhound with you for that spontaneous trip to Atlanta. The one who kept your secrets during your roughest years. The bonds you built were real. The history was sacred. But the present no longer feels aligned.

I had to face that truth in my own life. There was someone I once considered my sister-friend. We had history. Decades of it. She knew my childhood stories. I knew her grown woman trauma. For years, we showed up for each other. And then one day, I noticed I was the only one still showing up.

I made excuses. She's busy. She's going through something. She's overwhelmed. I sent the check-in texts. I made the invitations. I extended the grace. At some point, it stopped being grace and started being self-betrayal.

Letting her go didn't mean the memories disappeared. It didn't mean I stopped loving her. It meant I finally realized I was clinging to something that only I was still holding onto.

Releasing people without anger is a grown woman's superpower. You do not need a dramatic exit. You do not need to post about it. You do not need to beg for understanding. You simply stop watering what is no longer growing.

The silence that follows might feel sharp at first. It might feel like rejection. Over time, that same silence becomes sacred. It becomes your space to breathe. It becomes the doorway through which new friendships can enter. Friendships that see the version of you that exists right now. No, not the high school version. Not the party girl version. Not the corporate climb version. The now-you.

This season is not asking for more performances. It is asking for more presence. You deserve friendships that nourish you, not deplete you. You deserve relationships where your needs are not dismissed as too much, or your wins are not met with silent competition. You deserve to feel seen, heard, and chosen without having to chase, beg, or shrink.

It might look like no longer texting someone who only responds when they want something. It might mean not showing up to every event out of obligation. It might look like saying no to the friend who only calls when they are in a crisis, never just to check in. It might look like finally saying, "I love you, but this no longer feels good to me."

You are not too old to find new friends. You are not too late to start over. You are not too far gone to demand mutual energy and emotional safety. Let this be your turning point. Let this be the moment you stop performing for connections that do not perform for you. Let this be the chapter where you release the fantasy of who people were supposed to be, and instead make peace with who they really are.

Let them go. Let them do what they do. Let yourself rest. What comes next will meet you where you are, not where you had to shrink yourself to be. Take a moment here.

What you have just read might have brought up names, memories, old heartbreaks, or unresolved tensions. That is okay. Let it rise. Let it speak. Let it reveal what you no longer want to carry. You do not need another explanation. You do not need their permission. You only need your own honesty and the willingness to choose yourself.

In the next section, we will move from reflection to realignment. You will take all of this truth and turn it into action. You will check in on the relationships that matter, the ones that drain you, the ones that deserve a second look, and the ones that need to be retired for your peace. You already know what is not working. Now it is time to honor what is.

Let's begin.

Imagine this: you send a text to someone you've known for years. There's no emergency, and no ask. It is just a simple, heartfelt check-in. Maybe you saw a funny meme or heard a song that reminded you of that time y'all drove to New Orleans with $40 and a prayer. You wait for a reply. A few hours pass, then a day, then a week. You scroll up through the thread and realize your messages are doing all the heavy lifting. Blue bubble after blue bubble, and suddenly, the silence feels louder than any argument. You start to wonder if you've done something wrong, if they're okay, or if you've just quietly slipped off their priority list.

You begin to make excuses. Maybe they're overwhelmed. Maybe they meant to reply but got distracted. Maybe this is just how grown-up friendships look now. Or maybe it's time to stop justifying relationships that no longer meet you where you are.

Now picture this. You're having dinner with someone you love deeply, someone who has walked with you through major chapters of your life. The food is good, the setting is familiar, and at first, the conversation flows. Then you bring up something that matters to you, such as a new project, a personal breakthrough, or a major pivot you're finally ready to share. Suddenly, things shift. They nod in that polite, distracted way, give you a vague "that's interesting," then quickly steer the conversation back to themselves. You sit through the rest of the meal, present but disconnected. You don't feel attacked or mistreated. You just feel unseen. Not criticized, but also not celebrated. It is not loud enough to be called a conflict, but it is quiet enough to feel like a distance. That kind of emotional erosion is the hardest to name. It's when you realize that the version of yourself they once knew and connected with is no longer the version they're interested in knowing now.

Maybe you've carried that "pick me" energy into the workplace without even realizing it. You stayed late when no one asked, took on extra projects to prove your worth, laughed at jokes that weren't funny, and softened your voice in meetings to avoid sounding "too aggressive." You learned how to shape-shift into the person you thought would be most acceptable, someone who wouldn't ruffle feathers, and someone who would be liked. You morphed into a version of yourself that was palatable, all in the hope that someone would see you, choose you, promote you. At the end of the day, you went home emotionally exhausted, drained not by the workload but by the effort it took to wear the mask.

The real you barely got any oxygen. The truth is, when you're constantly contorting to be liked, you attract people who are only connected to your performance. It's only when you finally let your guard down that you allow your full self to show up. Your voice, your values, your edge, and your softness will be what the right people will begin to recognize you. You stop performing, and the right opportunities and relationships find their way to you, not because you chased them, but because you were finally rooted enough to be seen as you are.

Now imagine something even more radical. You decide to let all of that go. You stop initiating conversations that feel like work. You stop checking in on people who only show up when they're in need. You no longer rearrange your calendar to make room for connections that feel more like obligation than joy. Something inside you releases the pressure to maintain what is no longer mutual.

Then, almost without trying, you find yourself with more time. Your emotional bandwidth expands. You begin to notice how quiet it feels different now. The silence that once triggered anxiety now feels like rest. There is no rush to fix what is not broken, because it was never your job to carry those connections alone. You start to attract people who see you clearly in your now. There are people who honor your growth. They could be people who may not talk to you every week, but when they do, it feels like deep water. With them, there is no performance, just presence.

This is the midlife clarity you've earned. You no longer need every friendship to last forever. You only need to trust your ability to discern which ones are still worthy of your emotional investment.

## Cultivating Midlife Friendships That Nourish

Now that you've created space to release relationships that no longer serve you, you might wonder how to find new ones. I'm talking about authentic connections that feel nourishing, not tiring. Midlife friendships can be just as rich and meaningful as those we had in our youth, but they often look different. They are fewer in number, deeper in quality, and more intentional. They are less about proximity and more about purpose.

Research confirms this. A systematic review in *Frontiers in Psychology* from January 2023 examined nearly forty adult friendship studies over two decades. It found that the quality of adult friendships, not just the number, has a strong positive correlation with well-being across the PERMA model (positive emotion, engagement, relationships, meaning, accomplishment) (Baumeister, R. F., & Leary, M. R., 2023). Another study, published in the *International Journal of Psychology* last year, found that adults, especially women over 50, who have three or more close friends, report significantly better self-rated health than those without strong friendships (Chopik, W. J., & Oh, J., 2024). Simon Sinek even referred to friendship as the "ultimate biohack," noting that close confidants reduce stress, protect mental health, and can extend lifespan.

Friendships in midlife also fill essential emotional roles. A Swiss study comparing friendship networks in the 1970s and 2010s found that participation in non-kin relationships increased significantly, showing that later in life we intentionally invest more in chosen bonds (van Tilburg, T. G., & Broese van Groenou, M. I., 2022). Research has also shown that positive-quality friendships, characterized by trust, reliability, and autonomy, predict lower depressive symptoms and better self-rated health, even over extended periods (Stokes, J. E., & Moorman, S. M., 2024).

These insights underscore why midlife friendships matter more than ever. They protect mental health, enrich life satisfaction, and anchor us in our evolving identities. The challenge lies in locating connections without feeling like you're entering yet another competition in the youth-driven networking game.

**Where and How to Find Your People**

Some practical ways to discover meaningful connections in midlife include:

- **Join groups rooted in interest, not age**: Attend meetups or clubs that align with your passions, like photography, business growth masterminds, black women's poetry circles, or community education classes. Studies in *Time* suggest that repeating low-stakes interactions (like regular attendance at a café, class, or book club) builds deeper bonds over time (Walton, A. G. 2024, March 6).

- **Explore intergenerational communities**: Friendships with younger or older adults offer powerful benefits. They broaden perspectives and reduce loneliness, a critical consideration for adults over 50 (Fingerman, K. L., Huo, M., & Kim, K., 2023).

- **Form small, consistent circles**: You don't need large groups. Consider starting a small weekly or monthly gathering (coffee, bonfire, craft night) where consistency trumps scale. A Guardian article on the "friendship recession" suggests scheduling informal, recurring meetups to build deeper connections, especially among men (Wong, B. 2025, July 10).

- **Opt for quality over quantity**: Focus on people who enable autonomy, offer emotional support, and celebrate your wins, which are all qualities that research shows are vital to well-being.

- **Leverage your existing networks**: You already have history and shared language with some people from work, church, alumni circles, or former client groups. Start by inviting a few to a local brunch, a museum afternoon, or a walking group. Familiar foundations can open the door to renewed connection.

**Let This Be Your Invitation**

Midlife is not a friendship death sentence. It is an invitation to redesign your relational life with intention. You've already done the heavy lifting of letting go. Now you get to build. You deserve friendships that affirm, nurture, and uplift. Ones that honor the life you're living, not the one you left behind.

**Reflection: Respecting Boundaries and Releasing What No Longer Serves**

Now that you've walked through the emotional terrain of evolving relationships, it's time to bring this awareness inward and begin practicing what it means to release with intention, rather than guilt. This part of the journey is not about being cold or cutting people off for sport. It is about choosing your peace and honoring the version of yourself that no longer thrives in spaces that ask you to shrink.

One of the first steps is learning how to set boundaries with yourself. This may sound strange at first, but many of us were taught to bend, stretch, and overextend long before we ever learned how to protect our own energy. Take a moment to ask yourself where you might be ignoring your own discomfort. Are you continuing to show up for people out of obligation instead of alignment? Are you giving grace in places where you are no longer receiving basic respect? There is power in noticing the ways you betray your own needs in the name of loyalty. Choosing to protect your peace might look like not answering the phone when you're emotionally depleted. It might mean resisting the urge to initiate a conversation that leaves you feeling empty. It might mean recognizing that rest is also a boundary, and not every call or crisis requires your immediate involvement.

As you begin to make these internal shifts, practice letting people be who they are. This may sound simple, but it is one of the hardest things to do when your heart still holds onto a certain version of someone. People change. Circumstances will shift. The connection you once shared may no longer reflect the reality of your current needs. You do not have to keep watering a relationship that only grows resentment. When someone shows you who they are in this season, believe them (thank you Maya Angelou). It does not mean you no longer care. It means you are paying attention. You are allowed to adjust your expectations. You are allowed to release the hope that they will become who you need. Acceptance is not the same as resignation. It is clarity in action.

It also helps to check in with yourself about the relationships you continue to maintain out of familiarity. Sometimes we confuse history with depth. Just because someone has known you the longest does not mean they know you best. In midlife, it becomes even more important to seek out connections that reflect your current self. It's the version of you that is growing, questioning, pivoting, healing. Start noticing who makes space for that. Who listens without judgment. Who affirms your growth, even if they do not fully understand it yet. These are the people who deserve your presence. These are the relationships where your authenticity is not just tolerated, it is welcomed.

Choosing reciprocity over performance is not selfish. It is sacred. You are not difficult for wanting to be seen. You are not too much for needing tenderness. You are not ungrateful for walking away from relationships that once felt safe but now feel suffocating. You are simply creating space. You want space for clarity and ease. You'll create space for connection that feels less like a proving ground and more like a homecoming.

Take a breath and remind yourself that not every relationship is meant to last forever. Some are seasonal. Some are situational. Some were never meant to follow you into this next chapter. Letting them go does not erase what was. It simply allows you to honor what is. This is your permission to let go, realign, and reclaim your time, joy, and emotional capacity. You are allowed to do all of that without a dramatic exit or a final conversation. This ain't playing out in front of a live studio audience. You can release with love and still choose yourself.

Let this be the season where you stop begging for understanding and start building your life around people who require no explanation. Let this be the chapter where you practice your peace out loud.

# CHAPTER 14

## Put Some Respect on Your Name (and Your Budget): Midlife finances, freedom, and finally investing in YOU

If you grew up in a household where talking about money was taboo, where budgeting was just code for "you can't have that," and where treating yourself was seen as selfish or indulgent, then I have news for you. Welcome to your midlife money reset. This chapter is here to help you unlearn all of that.

By now, you've likely worked hard, supported others, saved and spent, made some financial missteps, and gathered a whole lot of wisdom along the way. You've juggled mortgages, car notes, student loans, emergency room bills, and possibly helped your grown kids take their first shaky steps into adulthood. You may have built entire lives around your capacity to give and support. But now? This is your time to pause, assess, and boldly realign your money with the life you're creating, not the one you were simply trying to survive in your 30s.

This is your permission slip to put your needs front and center, and back it up with a budget that doesn't just support your bills, but supports your *becoming*.

This is not about penny-pinching. It's not about being "good with money" by depriving yourself of anything beautiful or soft. I am advocating for quite the opposite. I want you to buy that luxury item or take that fabulous trip. The auto knee-jerk reaction of "I can't afford all that" might not be true. Your financial situation right now might reflect your priorities from a past era. There could be some things you are automatically throwing money at that are not as important as they once were. This is about creating a financial plan that reflects your current values, brings you peace of mind, and funds your future. In other words, your midlife budget isn't about cutting back. It's about leveling up, with intention.

## Budgeting as a Boundary

Your budget should be a boundary, not a burden. It's a tool to protect your time, your energy, and your vision. It should answer to you, not to other people's expectations. Instead of saying "I can't afford that," start asking, "Is this aligned with the life I'm building now?" When your money flows toward your values, it works harder for you, and it feels better, too.

Rather than guilt-tripping yourself over past financial mistakes or impulse buys, ask yourself, "What did that experience teach me, and how can I pivot now?" The goal is not to punish yourself for where your money has gone in the past. The goal is to redirect to where it's going next. That's financial maturity.

When someone comes knocking with another "ask," whether it's a family member needing help or a friend planning a girls' trip you truly can't swing, instead of defaulting to yes or letting guilt drive the decision, ask yourself, "Have I budgeted for generosity this month? Is this in alignment with what I'm building for myself?"

You're allowed to say no to the purchase. You're also allowed to say yes to yourself.

## The Emotional Side of Spending

Money is rarely just math. It's emotional. Every swipe of the card, every automatic payment, every splurge, every sacrifice, all tell a story. Sometimes we spend money to self-soothe (hello Target runs). Sometimes we buy things we don't need to distract from the things we don't want to feel. Sometimes we avoid even looking at our accounts because deep down we're afraid of what it will confirm. This is the part that takes courage.

Midlife is the perfect time to get honest about your financial triggers, your patterns, and the money stories you inherited or internalized. Maybe you equate earning more with finally being "enough." Maybe you've worked so hard to build wealth for others that you don't even know how to invest in yourself. Maybe you've been the financial backbone for so long that the idea of redirecting funds toward your joy feels foreign, or even selfish. It's not selfish. It's overdue. If you haven't noticed by this point in the book, I am deliberately trying to reclaim and reframe the word "selfish". In my world, it doesn't have a negative connotation. It literally means you are looking for yourself, first and foremost.

You are no longer obligated to be the financial hero in everyone else's story. You are allowed to redirect that same brilliance, resourcefulness, and energy toward your own freedom. You can forgive yourself for what you didn't know. You can release the shame of past decisions. You can move forward now with clarity, not guilt.

## The Midlife Rebudget: A Fresh Start

Let's reimagine what your money can actually do for you in this next chapter. What if you allowed yourself to make decisions that reflect your growth and your boldest dreams?

Want less house? Sell it.

Want more help around the house? Hire it.

Want a sabbatical? Start saving for it.

Want to learn something new or launch something big? Fund it.

This is not about reckless spending. This is about realignment.

When you audit your spending, you might find you've been investing in habits, subscriptions, or routines that no longer reflect who you are. Maybe you're still paying for a lifestyle that fits the old you, but not the version of you who is leaning into freedom, midlife joy, and legacy.

Maybe you've never stopped to consider what luxury means to you because you've always assumed it was out of reach. But here's a secret: luxury doesn't have to mean designer bags or first-class tickets (although if that's your thing, go for it). Luxury might be a silent, slow morning to yourself. It might mean a massage membership. Maybe it is a meal delivery service that frees up your time. It can be a solo birthday trip you don't explain to anybody. Your vision of luxury can be your beautifully decorated home office. It most definitely can be you hiring a financial planner on your team, or investing in coaching or courses that help you grow.

Luxury is about ease. It's about choosing to make your life feel softer, more aligned, more nourishing. And yes, it can be budgeted for.

## Let's Talk About Money...Finally

For many women, especially those of us in Generation X, money was something we were taught to either fear, avoid, or keep quiet about. In many Black households, especially those rooted in working-class values, money wasn't discussed as a source of power or freedom. It was a source of tension. Talking about it made people uncomfortable. Asking for more made you look ungrateful. Dreaming too big was seen as unrealistic. The message was clear: be content, stay humble, and make do with what you already have.

In families where money was tight, contentment wasn't just a value. It was a survival strategy. Many of our mothers and grandmothers didn't have access to wealth-building tools or professional advancement, and they often worked twice as hard for half as much. Their focus was on keeping the lights on, feeding the family, and passing on strength. They didn't talk about investing or personal finance because they weren't allowed the luxury of learning it. Hell, it wasn't until the 1974 Equal Credit Opportunity Act that women were legally allowed to open their own bank accounts, without having a male relative co-sign for it. What they knew, they learned through very hard experiences. That legacy left many of us equipped with resilience, but not necessarily with financial clarity.

Recent research backs this up. A 2023 Cambridge review of financial literacy in the U.S. confirmed that Black adults, especially Black women, continue to face disparities in financial knowledge and access to wealth-building tools, in part due to long-standing systemic inequities (Moya Vu, S., et al. 2023). Another 2021 report from the *TIAA Institute* found that Black and Hispanic women report lower financial confidence, often due to a lack of tailored education and institutional trust (Clark, R., Davis, H., & Mitchell, O. S., 2021). These aren't character flaws. These are structural realities, and they show why the emotional baggage many of us carry around money is not just personal. It's generational.

That internal conflict often gets even more complicated for those of us who were raised in service-oriented professions. I had to wrestle with it myself. As a former educator, I spent years operating under the belief that teaching was a "calling." We weren't supposed to enter the profession for the money or hoping to get rich. In fact, there was a kind of nobility in not caring about salary, as if the sacrifice itself was a badge of honor. We were conditioned to believe that loving the kids and doing good work meant money shouldn't matter.

Sadly, for a long time, I accepted that script. I dismissed financial ambition. I downplayed any desire to "want more". But once I left the classroom and stepped into a new season of leadership and entrepreneurship, I had to face the truth: I do like money. I like what it provides. I like what it protects. I like what it makes possible.

When people say, "Money can't buy happiness," I disagree. It may not buy happiness outright, but it does purchase options. Those options are often what create ease, freedom, and joy. According to that same 2024 *Pew Research Center* report, a majority of Black Americans define financial success not by wealth accumulation alone, but by freedom from debt and the ability to make meaningful life choices. The study revealed that financial peace and the freedom to enjoy life were more central than just the size of a paycheck.

Money is a tool. It creates space. It creates rest. It buys time. It allows for therapy, travel, sabbaticals, medical care, freedom from toxic workplaces, and time to explore your creativity. It allows you to say yes to yourself and no to people or patterns that drain you.

This kind of financial clarity isn't just about luxury. It's about mental health. A 2024 *Forbes* report highlighted how financial strain impacts the emotional well-being of Black women, affecting not only stress levels but also their confidence and career advancement (Marcus, B., 2024). The study noted that women who feel financially secure are more likely to advocate for themselves, set boundaries at work, and invest in personal development.

The effects ripple into our relationships, too. A 2023 *PMC* study on midlife couples found that ongoing financial strain was associated with reduced intimacy and lower life satisfaction over time (Lee, H. Y., & Stevens, D., 2023). When your money is misaligned with your values, it doesn't just show up in your bank account. It shows up in your relationships, your health, and your daily peace.

It is time to reclaim your narrative. You are not selfish for wanting more. You are self-aware. You are not greedy for desiring ease. You are healing from years of carrying everyone else's needs while quietly ignoring your own. You are not wrong for wanting to earn more, rest more, and enjoy the fruits of your labor without apology.

Say it clearly. You like money. You want more of it. You know how to use it. You are ready to fund a life that reflects the person you've become, not just the one who had to "make do." Money isn't the whole story, but it can fund the chapter you're writing next.

## From Paycheck to Purpose: Turning Free Time into a Freedom Stream

Midlife isn't just about maintaining what you've already built. It is the perfect time to ask yourself what still needs to be created. If you've found yourself daydreaming about launching a podcast, teaching a skill, selling a product, or finally pursuing that idea you've tucked away for years, this is your moment. That persistent curiosity, that quiet nudge to explore something new, is not a distraction. It is direction.

If people often tell you, "You're really good at that," or if you find yourself giving away advice, services, or insight for free, you may already be sitting on a skillset or idea that could become your next income stream. Many of us have untapped talents or dreams that have been buried under responsibility, family life, and the daily grind. Now that life is shifting and your calendar may have more flexibility, you finally have time to ask, "What can I build that truly fulfills me?"

This is exactly how it started for me.

While working full-time in a corporate role, I noticed something. People, especially midlife women, kept coming to me with the same questions. They wanted advice on career transitions, LinkedIn strategies, resume revamps, and navigating professional pivots with confidence. These conversations felt natural to me. I had been through those transitions myself. What began as casual chats and side conversations slowly started to reveal a pattern.

I realized that people kept coming to me for something I didn't just enjoy, I was good at it. A light bulb went off. I had already built this knowledge through lived experience, and I could package it in a way that served others and supported me. What began as informal guidance turned into coaching, speaking, and eventually, the launch of my podcast and the foundation of my business.

It did not require quitting my job or taking on a huge financial risk. It began with a choice. I made a decision to treat my ideas as valuable. That shift in mindset allowed everything else to follow.

Once I made that decision, my habits changed. I stopped wasting so much time scrolling social media and started carving out space to develop my own voice and vision. I began seeking out guidance from other podcasters and online coaches. I studied how they showed up, what tools they used, how they structured their time, and how they turned knowledge into income. I took notes. I asked questions. I invested in low-cost courses and learned by doing.

The truth is, there are resources all around you when you are ready to pay attention. You just have to shift your focus from consumption to creation.

Your version of a side hustle might look different. Maybe you're great at organizing and could build a service around that. Maybe people are always complimenting your writing, your style, your event planning, or your ability to explain things clearly. Maybe you've always wanted to teach, create, or build something that reflects your passions. The ideas don't have to be perfect right away. They just need space to be explored.

If you're curious about turning your ideas into income, here are a few ways to get started:

**Start by taking inventory of your natural strengths.** Think about what people consistently come to you for. Ask yourself what you do with ease that others find challenging. Look at your own journey for clues. Chances are, you've overcome something that others are still trying to figure out.

Here are some tips to get you started:

**Create space to build your ideas.** Designate time in your week to brainstorm, research, write, or test new things. Even an hour a day can make a big difference. Use this time as a creative sanctuary, not another to-do list item. Let it be exciting.

**Find people who are already doing what you want to do.** Learn from them. Follow their content. Listen to their podcasts. Join their workshops or communities. You do not have to reinvent the wheel. You just have to be willing to learn.

**Test your ideas before you try to perfect them.** Offer your service to a few people for free or low cost in exchange for feedback. Watch how it feels. Notice what lights you up and what drains you. Let experience be your guide, not perfectionism.

**Notice where your time is leaking.** If you find yourself saying you don't have time to build something new, look at how much time you spend scrolling or consuming other people's content. You have time. The question is whether you are giving it to your own dreams or everyone else's.

Fear will try to talk you out of it. You might hear yourself saying, "Who am I to do this?" or "It's too late to start now." Another excuse I hear over and over is that the market is too saturated. Too many people are already providing the services you want to lean into. Do not let that stop you. A so-called saturated market just means it is a product or service that is in high demand. If people are still showing up everyday at the nail salon, car wash, hiring event planners, and t-shirt printers, that means there is high demand for those products and services. By the way, remember that podcast you've been dreaming of launching? You don't have to break the internet. You just need a tiny slice of the World Wide Web to tune to your platform.

These are not just cute stories. They are facts. You are not too old, too behind, or too late. You are experienced. You are resourceful. You are ready. You've already spent decades showing up for everyone else. Now is the time to show up for yourself.

Whether your idea brings in a few hundred dollars a month or becomes a foundation for a future business, you owe it to yourself to explore what's possible. This is not about chasing hustle culture. It is about creating freedom on your own terms.

Midlife is not the end of opportunity. It is the beginning of alignment.

**Mind Mapping Your Midlife Magic**

Discover the skills, talents, and passions that could become your next income stream.

If I've got your attention and you're curious about what hidden talent you could monetize, take a few minutes to do this activity. You don't need to reinvent yourself to create something new. You already have experiences, gifts, and knowledge that are valuable. This mind-mapping activity will help you gently uncover the areas of your life where talent meets opportunity, so you can begin imagining what a side hustle or career pivot might look like.

**Step 1: Start With You**

Write your name in the center of a blank page or notebook. Draw a circle around it. This is your starting point.

From that center, draw 4 lines outward like branches. Label them:

1.  What Comes Naturally

2.  What People Ask Me For

3.  What I've Learned the Hard Way

4.  What I Daydream About

## Branch 1: What Comes Naturally

List the things you do with ease. These are often your quiet superpowers. List things others may find difficult, but you enjoy or can do on autopilot.

Example: organizing chaos, making people feel seen, writing with clarity, problem-solving, public speaking, designing spaces, cooking, storytelling.

**Prompt:**

What do I do so well that I forget it's a skill?

## Branch 2: What People Ask Me For

List the things friends, family, coworkers, or even strangers regularly come to you for. These often point to talents that others already see in you.

Example: reviewing resumes, offering relationship advice, providing business feedback, offering tech help, tutoring, styling, and wellness tips.

**Prompt:**

What do people trust me to help them with—even when I'm not trying?

## Branch 3: What I've Learned the Hard Way

Think about your journey. Include the setbacks, pivots, breakthroughs, or survival stories you carry. These lessons often become the foundation for service or storytelling work.

Example: career transitions, caregiving, burnout recovery, divorce healing, raising children, navigating loss, starting over.

**Prompt:**

What have I overcome that others are still trying to figure out?

## Branch 4: What I Daydream About

This is your chance to let your imagination run. What do you wish you had more time for? What excites you? What would you try if fear, time, or money weren't holding you back?

Example: launching a podcast, starting a small product line, hosting workshops, writing a book, opening a retreat space, becoming a coach.

### Prompt:

What keeps tugging at me, no matter how many times I try to ignore it?

### Bringing It All Together

Look at your branches. Circle the items that feel the most energizing, exciting, or doable. Don't worry about whether they're "realistic." This is about curiosity and clarity.

Then ask:

- What do these ideas have in common?
- Which ones could I start exploring with just a few hours a week?
- Which ones could become a service, product, or creative outlet?

Write one idea you feel most drawn to right now, and one small action you could take in the next 7 days to explore it further.

### Example:

Idea: I love helping people prepare for interviews and rewrite their resumes.

Action Step: Reach out to a friend who's job hunting and offer to help them prep. Ask for feedback.

## One more thought

This exercise is not about building a business overnight. It's about reconnecting with what makes you *you*. You could be using it to create something that brings purpose and possibly profit. Let your answers guide your next brave step.

Your next opportunity might already be sitting inside of you, waiting for permission to grow.

## A New Kind of Spending Power

By this stage in life, you are likely earning more than you ever have. Or perhaps you're working less, but finally have more control over your time. Either way, you have power. The question is: where is it going?

A grown woman's budget says: I choose how I live now. I choose how I treat myself. I choose what matters. That means you might spend less on fast fashion and more on travel. You might stop saying yes to every family obligation and start saying yes to a dream you've put off for a decade. You might be surprised how affordable your dream life actually is, once you stop spending money trying to keep up with a version of you that no longer exists.

## Essentials vs. Emotional Spending Diagnostic

You need a grown-up check-in to realign your money with your midlife values. Let's be real: the way we spend money tells the truth, even when we don't say it out loud. This is your chance to get honest about what's essential, what's emotional, and what's aligned. You're not here to live a life of guilt and grind. You're here to build a life that feels as good as it looks, and that starts with understanding where your money's going and why.

We are going to walk through a few categories of your spending that might need some overhauling. Remember, there is no judgment here. You are looking for places where money is flying out the window. It's an opportunity to redirect those dollars toward the bigger luxuries you deserve. This exercise isn't about restriction. It's about reclamation. We are not shrinking. We are sharpening.

## CATEGORY 1: ESSENTIAL SPENDING

These are the non-negotiables. Rent or mortgage. Groceries. Health insurance. Transportation. Bills. Anything that keeps your life functional, stable, and safe.

That said, some of us have turned "essential" into "excessive" without even noticing. You might be paying for a home that's too big for your needs now, or holding onto two streaming services you forgot you had because your grown kids used to watch cartoons on them. Sometimes, we inherit habits from our survival years and keep paying for things that no longer reflect our reality.

Yes, you need food. But do you need $800 worth of takeout when half your fridge ends up being a science experiment? Yes, you need shelter. But do you need 3,700 square feet of rooms you never sit in anymore?

This is not judgment. This is clarity.

### Reflection Prompt:

What parts of my "essential" spending are leftovers from a life I no longer live? Where could I simplify, not to deprive myself, but to create space for what I actually want?

## CATEGORY 2: EMOTIONAL SPENDING

Let's talk about that retail therapy. There is the "I had a hard week" Amazon cart. Then you have the moment when you hit "Buy Now" just to feel something. What about the Target run where you went in for paper towels and came out with two throw pillows, a new water bottle, and a scented candle you didn't even like? Yeah, that was me, too, once upon a time.

Emotional spending isn't always loud. Sometimes it's sneaky. It might show up as saying yes to a brunch you can't afford because you don't want to feel left out. It might be buying gifts for people out of guilt instead of love. It might be overspending on your appearance, not because it brings you joy, but because you're trying to meet someone else's standards.

Here's the truth: money can't fix your mood long term. That dopamine hit wears off, and then you're left with buyer's remorse and a stack of unopened boxes. This is not about cutting off all pleasure. It's about knowing the difference between a joy-filled treat and a bandage for an unspoken wound.

**Reflection Prompt:**

Where am I using money to manage my emotions instead of facing them? What feelings am I trying to buy my way out of? What can I do instead that actually nourishes me?

## CATEGORY 3: ALIGNMENT SPENDING

This is the money that speaks your name. The stuff that feeds your spirit, stretches your vision, or makes your life feel just a little more luxurious in the ways that matter to *you*.

It might be a solo trip with ocean views and no one asking you what's for dinner. It might be a course that reignites a dream. It might be a cleaning service that gives you three hours of peace and hands you back your weekend. It might be a therapist or life coach who helps you unpack years of survival mode and teaches you how to thrive.

This is the spending that reflects the version of you who is no longer asking for permission to enjoy her life. It is intentional. It is unapologetic. It is deeply personal. It is not about impressing others. It's about honoring yourself. Alignment spending may not be the loudest item on your budget, but it should be the most sacred.

**Reflection Prompt:**

What are the things, services, or experiences that make me feel more whole, more rested, more seen? Where have I been playing small with my money because I was afraid to put me first?

**Final Reflection: Your Grown-Up Budgeting Energy**

This is the part where you sit with what you've learned, not with shame, but with power. You've worked too hard to build a life that doesn't fit. You've earned the right to talk about money, to want money, to use money. Money is not just for paying bills, but to build beauty, ease, rest, and joy.

Having money doesn't make you less spiritual, less kind, or less grounded. It gives you choices. It gives you space. It gives you time. Wanting more isn't selfish. Wasting it on things that don't reflect your values *is*. You don't need anyone's approval to start budgeting for joy. You just need your own permission.

**Now Try This:**

- Identify three spending habits that no longer serve you and make a plan to phase them out over the next 90 days.

- Choose one new habit that supports the life you're creating. Let it be something joyful, aligned, or luxurious.

- Name one belief about money that you are ready to release. Then, write a new belief to replace it.

This is your money. This is your life. Make it count, pun intended.

# CHAPTER 15

## You Don't Have to Do This Alone: Creating Your Community of Fellow Reinventors and Truth-Tellers

S omewhere along the way, many of us internalized the message that strong women do it all on their own. We somehow felt that asking for help made us weak. We should know how to manage everything ourselves, navigate career changes, parent grown kids, care for aging parents, process trauma, keep a household together, and still show up for everyone else. We equated independence with isolation and got really good at performing like we had it all together.

Midlife brings us face-to-face with the truth. That myth is exhausting, and more importantly, it's a lie. You do not have to do this alone. This chapter is a reclaiming. It is still part of that growing permission slip. It is your reminder that having a community is not a luxury. Build your village and then lean into it. Your village is a life source, especially now and especially here.

Midlife reinvention is not meant to be a solo mission. If you're in the middle of rebuilding your life, healing from heartbreak, starting a business, grieving a parent, navigating menopause, or just trying to hear your own voice over all the noise, community will carry you farther, faster, and with more grace than grit alone ever could.

Read this carefully. Needing people is not a flaw. Knowing you need people is wisdom.

## When You've Been Carrying Too Much Alone

Maybe this will sound familiar. You can't remember the last time you asked for help. You're the one everyone turns to, but you rarely open up. Your to-do list is overflowing, but your support circle is shrinking. You've stopped dreaming because just getting through the day takes all your energy.

You might be holding the world up for everyone else, but who's holding space for you? I have worked with countless individuals who didn't even realize how isolated they had become. They were managing caregiving for their aging parents, navigating the emotional whiplash of adult children, holding down full-time careers, and dealing with health shifts of their own. They were barely managing all of that, and silently. It doesn't have to be that way.

In one of my podcast episodes, my dear friend Chaundy Satterwhite shared her journey of becoming a full-time caregiver for her mother. Being thrust into the caregiver role was sudden and confusing for her. She had to create a village of support to help her through an extremely challenging period of taking care of her ailing mother. The whole experience inspired her to launch her own business, GenGap Living, to help others navigate the caregiver journey with less overwhelm and more dignity for their aging parents. The calls started rolling in when people heard her story. There were several women in midlife who suddenly found themselves in the same role of caretaker with no manual, no map, and no emotional support. What started as a teachable moment became a movement. Chandy turned her experience into a resource for others, and she now leads families through the very process that once overwhelmed her. That is the power of storytelling and the beautiful power of community.

**The Science Is Clear. We Need Each Other to Heal.**

Over the last five years, research has confirmed what we already know in our bones. Social connection is essential for our health, happiness, and longevity. Here's what the data tells us.

1.  A 2020 meta-analysis published in *American Psychologist* found that strong social relationships improve survival by 50 percent, comparable to quitting smoking and better than physical activity or weight loss (Holt-Lunstad, 2020).

2.  The Harvard Study of Adult Development, one of the longest studies on happiness ever conducted, concluded in 2023 that close relationships, more than money or fame, are what keep people happy throughout their lives.

3.  A 2022 study in *The Journals of Gerontology* showed that social isolation in older adults significantly increases risk for cognitive decline, depression, and mortality.

4.  The National Academies of Sciences, Engineering, and Medicine (2020) reported that more than one-third of adults aged 45 and older feel lonely, and nearly one-fourth of adults aged 65 and older are socially isolated.

5.  A 2023 study in *Frontiers in Psychology* showed that participation in intentional community support groups, especially among women over 40, resulted in higher reported life satisfaction, decreased stress levels, and increased motivation toward personal goals.

In plain terms, connection heals. Disconnection harms. We saw this vividly during the pandemic. The isolation wasn't just inconvenient, but deeply emotionally brutal. Many of us lost more than routines. We lost rituals, support systems, hugs, conversations, church gatherings, brunches, and breathers. That loneliness? It wasn't just felt. It was lived. And it reminded us how much we need community. You remember how that felt. That's why now, in this midlife season, it's time to be intentional about rebuilding your circle.

## You Get to Choose Who's Around You Now

One of the greatest gifts of midlife is discernment. You've lived enough to know who energizes you and who drains you. You've learned that there is a difference between being included and being seen. You know that surface-level brunch friends are not the same as the soul-deep truth-tellers. Even if you throw it way back to the late 1900s when you were school age, your friend group was likely formed out of geographical convenience. We hung out with the neighborhood kids in elementary school, and could walk to their houses when we wanted to play outside. Our high school lunch buddies were kids who had similar class schedules to our own. There wasn't a lot of choice involved. Our community just kind of fell into place based on our similar circumstances. Now is the time to choose community over crowd, and choose nourishment over noise. The people you surround yourself with in this next season will shape how far and how fully you rise. So get clear. Ask yourself these questions:

- Who makes me feel like my full self?
- Who challenges me to grow with love, not judgment?
- Who do I feel safe being messy and vulnerable with?
- Who holds space for my dreams, even the unfinished ones?

That is your community. Find them. You can also build them from scratch if you have to.

When I launched my podcast, it was because I couldn't find the kind of conversations I needed. I yearned for conversations that honored Black womanhood and midlife pivots. I was in the middle of my own career reinvention, so I needed that level of community too. There were so many challenges I'd faced, so I sought emotional healing without apology. I decided to build the space I needed. Wouldn't you know, thousands of other women showed up too.

That's what happens when you choose authenticity over performance. Your people can finally find you.

## Healing Happens in Community

In another powerful episode of my podcast, I sat down with sisters and co-authors Dr. Denetria Phlegm and Qiana S. Compton, whose book *Perspectives* recounts their deeply personal journey through trauma, silence, and eventual liberation. Their story begins with a family tragedy that left invisible scars, shaping how they navigated adulthood, relationships, motherhood, and even their sense of self. For years, they kept their pain private, like so many of us do. There was a shared belief that if you don't talk about it, maybe it won't hurt as much.

But pain has a way of leaking through the cracks. And healing? Healing demands a voice.

Instead of remaining quiet, they chose to share their truth publicly. Writing *Perspectives* wasn't just cathartic for them. It became a mirror for others, especially Black women, who saw pieces of their own stories reflected in the pages. That's the radical power of storytelling. It doesn't just release the storyteller. It liberates the listener, too.

That's what community does. A supportive community creates safe containers where truth can live and grow. It says, "You're not crazy or broken. You're not alone." Healing in community means someone is there to witness your pain without judgment and hold space for your transformation without rushing it.

As Dr. Phlegm said during our conversation, "The best thing you can give your kids is a healed parent." That line stopped me in my tracks. Because for so many midlife women, especially those of us who were taught to prioritize others at all costs, healing can feel like a luxury. But it's not. It's a necessity.

Let me also add this: the best thing you can give *yourself* is a circle that holds you while you heal. That is your sister circle. It is a truth-telling space, or a no-mask-needed zone. Whether it's a group chat, a book club, a support group, or a tight-knit group of friends who remind you who you are on your hardest days, the healing accelerates when done in the presence of others.

You don't have to process the hard stuff alone. You were never meant to.

## What to Look for in a Midlife Circle

This isn't about finding a crowd. We are not worried about being popular and liked by the masses. It's about curating a circle. It should be a sacred, intentional circle.

Here's what that might include: the *validation* that your story matters and that someone, somewhere, is waiting to hear it. Your words might be the very thing that gives them hope. It includes *support*, the kind that shows up when you speak your truth and discover the right people don't retreat. They actually lean in closer. It's also about *growth*, the kind that comes from being challenged, celebrated, and encouraged in ways that reignite your inner spark. There is *joy* as well. This includes deep belly laughs with people who just get you, reminding you that laughter truly is medicine. *Accountability* is also essential, where your community holds you to the vision of your highest self, even during moments when you lose sight of who that is. These elements form the foundation of a community that doesn't just surround you. It uplifts, heals, and helps you become more of who you're meant to be.

This is not about rescuing others or saving broken friendships. This is about designing and nurturing a circle that reflects where you're going, not where you've been.

**Community Isn't Found. It's Built.**

If you're looking around and realizing your circle is too small, too shallow, or too distant, you're not alone. Many of us drifted apart during the pandemic. Others of us outgrew old dynamics. For some, life simply shifted, and we forgot to keep watering the friendships we wanted to keep. It's not too late.

Start where you are. Build what you need, brick by brick, and conversation by conversation. That woman you always talk to after yoga class? Invite her for coffee. That old friend you've been meaning to call? Reach out today. That online group you've been lurking in? Introduce yourself.

Community doesn't require ten people. Sometimes two ride-or-dies are enough. The point is not quantity. It's resonance. It's mutuality. It's safety. Let go of performing. Let go of perfect. Show up as you. The right people will meet you there.

Now that you've reflected on the why and the who, it's time to begin designing your midlife community with care and intention. This next section will guide you through that process, helping you evaluate your current circle, identify what you most need, and begin rebuilding a support system that meets you where you are.

**Activity: Mapping Your Midlife Support System**

You've spent a lifetime being the dependable one. The fixer. The steady hand. The shoulder everyone else leans on. Somewhere along the way, you might have convinced yourself that your strength came from being able to do it all on your own.

But here's the truth. You are allowed to need. You are allowed to ask. You are allowed to want more than survival.

This activity is not about listing names just for the sake of it. It's about taking an honest look at the relationships in your life and beginning to build the kind of intentional, supportive community that can hold you through this next chapter.

As you move through the journal prompts and exercises, give yourself permission to be reflective. Be honest enough to feel what comes up. This is not about shame or regret. It's about clarity and care. You are worthy of support. You are worthy of connection. You are worthy of a circle that sees you, supports you, and stretches with you. Let's start creating it on purpose.

**Reflective Journal Prompts**

1.  Who are the five people I can truly be myself with right now?

2.  What kind of support do I most need in this season?

3.  When was the last time I reached out for help or support? What happened?

4.  Am I surrounded by people who make me feel seen and celebrated, or judged and invisible?

5.  What kind of friend or community member do I want to be for others?

**Action Steps**

- **Support Circle Mapping**

   Create 3 columns: "People who support me," "People I support," and "People I want to reconnect or go deeper with". Fill in as many names as they come to mind.

- **Reach Out Challenge**

   Pick one name from the third column. This week, send a message, schedule a walk, or leave a voice note. Let them know they've been on your mind.

- **Community Visioning**

   Imagine your ideal support circle.

   ○ How often do you gather?

   ○ What do you talk about?

○   What values hold you together?

Now, brainstorm one step to make that group real. Start a group chat. Host a meetup. Join a book club.

**Final Word. Connection Is the Cure.**

Midlife isn't just about letting go. It's about letting in. Let in the support. Let in the healing. Let in the joy. Let in the people who see the real you and still choose to stay. Doing it alone is no longer brave. It's just unnecessary. Let this be the chapter where you stop pretending you have it all together and start building the kind of circle that can help you hold it all.

# CHAPTER 16

## This is My Next Chapter, And I'm Writing It My Way: A Guided Blueprint to Design the Career, Home, and Life You Actually Want Now

At some point in midlife, you wake up and realize you've been the supporting actress in everyone else's movie. You've played the roles: daughter, mother, partner, employee, leader, caregiver, Girl Scout cookie coordinator, last-minute school project hero, office therapist, PTO volunteer. Your rap sheet in these supporting roles is stacked. While some of those roles were beautiful and life-shaping, you may not have had much say in the script. You went along to get along, and that is okay. Maybe it was what you needed to do, or better yet, who you needed to be at those points in your history. However, now, you are looking forward.

This chapter is about flipping the script and writing a role that finally feels like you. I'm not just talking about a reboot. You are about to make a reinvention, my dear. We don't have to wait for a breakdown to make a breakthrough. Your midlife experience does not have to be a crisis. You have the power to make this your bold, creative act and upgrade.

By the time you've made it through the earlier chapters of this book, you've likely seen your own reflection in stories like my cousin Tina's, who turned an unexpected layoff in her 60's mind you, into the launch of her own permanent jewelry business. Maybe you related to Janelle's journey, who was learning to pay her first bill at age 38 after leaving a life and marriage that no longer fit. Or perhaps it was Angela, who created an entire clean beauty line because her body and spirit demanded better care with quality ingredients. There was also the inspirational Sabrina, who launched a business from her hospital bed while recovering from a stem cell transplant. These are not women who had a neat five-year plan. These are women who got real about their truth, their timing, and their power.

This is where your blueprint begins.

### This Isn't a Drill, Sis. This Is Your Life

Midlife has a way of tapping you on the shoulder like, "Hey, we're doing this now." Whether it's a diagnosis, a job loss, a shift in your family structure, or just the quiet ache that says, "There's more," the invitation arrives whether you're ready or not.

So many of us say we're waiting for the perfect moment. Waiting until we lose ten pounds. Waiting until the kids are settled. Waiting until we have more energy, more clarity, more money, more support. I am truly guilty of all the above. Launching my podcast was something I wanted to put off because I felt like I needed to lose weight first. Looking back now, that feels ridiculous. However, now I think back to that past version of myself, and I have so much love and gratitude for her taking that bold step. She (I) wanted to put it off for a few months and pop out as someone different and more put together. She (I) wanted to hide a little longer, just to overthink the whole idea and possibly never do it, because it felt scary. But she didn't wait for someday. She took the leap from exactly where she was standing.

That mythical "someday" has stolen too many dreams. Someday is not a date on the calendar. Today is. You don't need permission. You need a plan. By the way, that plan just needs to get you moving one step at a time. It needs to get you unstuck and out of your own head. The big goal is further ahead, but you don't need to look at it too closely yet. For now, just move, with baby steps. Look at where you are today and ask yourself if you want to be in the exact same place, mentally, emotionally, physically, and financially one year from now. If the quick answer is no, then you have a glimpse of where your heart is leading you.

## You Already Have the Ingredients

Every late-night Google search, every time you helped someone else get their life together, every notebook full of ideas, every "you should be charging for this" text you got from friends… was all data. You've been collecting the receipts without even trying.

You've seen what it looks like when other women decided they were done being boxed in. You've felt the itch to do something different, even if you didn't know exactly what it was yet. You've already survived hard things. Now let's build from that resilience.

## The Reinvention Blueprint: Your Midlife Power Plan

This is not a mood board. It's not a Pinterest dream. This is your blueprint. Built on receipts, resilience, and realignment. You've already spent years collecting pieces of your identity. Now it's time to assemble them into something that actually fits you. Here is the breakdown of your midlife redesign blueprint.

## Career: The Remix

You remember the moment Mary J. Blige dropped the "My Life" album, don't you? It was raw, vulnerable, and soul-baring. That was a soundtrack for every woman trying to hold it together while quietly falling apart. That's what reinvention often feels like. You're rewriting the verses of your work life by deciding what stays, what gets cut, and what needs a whole new beat.

Maybe you've been the go-to expert at your job, but felt invisible when it came to promotions. Maybe you've mastered every classroom, boardroom, or virtual Zoom room they threw at you. Yet, something is still missing. You want your work to feel like alignment, not just survival.

My old colleague Tamara pivoted from education to entrepreneurship in her 50s, and it started with one simple realization: her skills weren't limited to one classroom or a school building. She could teach, coach, strategize, and you guessed it, she could charge for it. Just like that bootleg CD-copying hustle from back in the day, she repackaged what she already had and created something new and in demand.

*Ask Yourself:*

- What part of your work still excites you, and what part feels like AOL dial-up in a fiber-optic world?

- Are you climbing the wrong ladder, or is it time to build your own?

- What would it look like to earn with more freedom, flexibility, or purpose?

## Home: From MTV Cribs to Soul Sanctuary

Remember how obsessed we were with watching *MTV Cribs* in the early 2000s? Big closets, granite everything, jacuzzis in every corner. Now? Most of us would settle for a peaceful space with no clutter, no chaos, and a functioning washer that doesn't walk across the floor during the spin cycle.

Home in midlife isn't about showing off. It's about showing up for yourself. When I downsized from the suburban sprawl to a downtown apartment, it was less about square footage and more about energy. I wanted a place that didn't need me to keep performing. A soft place to land after hard days was the new goal. I let go of the rooms no one used and leaned into what I truly needed: sunlight, quiet, comfort, and a fridge stocked with fresh, ready-made meals (did I mention I don't cook much anymore?).

My cousin Tina turned her home into a creative studio and launched her business from within those comfy walls. Her life got bigger when her living space took on a dual purpose.

*Ask Yourself:*

- Does your home reflect who you are now, or who you were then?

- What are you holding onto out of guilt or habit?

- If your home could feel like a hug, what would need to change?

**Finances: Real Grown Woman Energy**

Remember when we used to joke about Sallie Mae like she was a frenemy we couldn't shake? Or how "mo' money, mo' problems" felt like a prophecy? Well, now, we're not quoting lyrics. We're looking at budgets, checking our 401(k), and trying to figure out how many streams of income it takes to sleep peacefully at night.

Midlife finances hit different. It's not because you suddenly become perfect with money, but because you start to really care where your dollars are going. You want investments, not just impulse buys. Legacy becomes far more important than just your lifestyle.

Angela got laid off and told herself, "Never again will I have just one stream of income." She built a beauty line from her kitchen and became her own safety net. She didn't wait for the perfect conditions. She just got started, one ingredient at a time.

*Ask Yourself:*

- Are your dollars aligned with your desires, or just your deadlines?

- What would financial freedom actually feel like for you?

- Are you building wealth, or just maintaining bills?

**Community: Find Your Living Single Crew**

We all watched *Living Single* like it was our actual friend group. You had your Khadijahs, your Regines, your Synclairs. Everybody wanted Maxine Shaw's confidence. There was joy, shade, ambition, and unwavering sisterhood. That's what a midlife community should feel like: soulful, supportive, and safe.

This isn't the season for performative friendships. You don't need anyone taking up space who doesn't also pour back into you. Janelle built her circle from scratch. After her divorce, trauma, and career changes, she created masterminds, clubhouse talks, and coaching circles that nourished her spirit and her highly successful real estate business. She didn't just wait for the right people. She became the right person and attracted her crew.

*Ask Yourself:*

- Who makes you feel seen, not just needed?

- Are your friendships reciprocal, or just nostalgic?

- Who do you need to love from a distance so you can love yourself more clearly?

**Joy: Back to the Essence**

Remember the vibe of Saturday morning cartoons, a bowl of cereal, and nowhere to be? Or when a good Anita Baker song could heal your whole middle school spirit? Joy wasn't complicated. It was just an easy presence.

Midlife joy isn't just about big vacations or Instagram aesthetics. It's about reclaiming the parts of you that got buried under productivity. It's about taking your pleasure seriously.

Joy looks like learning to skate again because you loved it at 13. Joy is picking up a paintbrush or dancing in the kitchen to SWV, singing off-key. Joy is reading a book with zero educational purpose.

It's laughter that reaches your belly. It's choosing peace even when you're not done fixing the mess.

*Ask Yourself:*

- What did joy look like before your life got so full of responsibility?

- What's the thing you keep saying you'll do "someday" that you could try this month?

- What joy have you delayed that you now need to prioritize like your peace depends on it?

**Start Where You Are**

The truth is, nobody ever feels completely ready. Readiness is a myth we were sold somewhere between college brochures and corporate onboarding. What's real is *willingness*. That is something you already have.

Janelle didn't wait until the timing was perfect, because it wasn't. She was recovering from a health crisis that left her body tired but her mind alive with new clarity. In the quiet moments between doctor visits and tears, she started dreaming of a coaching practice where women like her could finally feel seen. Her first step wasn't some big launch. It was opening a blank notebook and scribbling her truths.

Angela didn't have a fancy lab or startup money. She had a kitchen, a deep frustration with toxic ingredients, and a spiritual tug that said, "There has to be a better way." So she started mixing oils. Testing. Failing. Trying again. Before long, the same products she was making for herself became gifts for friends, and then sales for customers who didn't even know her story, but felt her magic in the jar.

Tina spent over 30 years perfecting her communication skills in a corporate setting, mentoring teams, and managing big campaigns.

When her job was eliminated, she didn't crumble. She got curious. She took what she already knew and created a niche jewelry business. Clients didn't care that she was starting over. They cared that she knew how to help them shine. Tina didn't go back to square one. She simply pivoted and took imperfect action.

Each of these women faced fear. Each started in less-than-ideal conditions. Each used what was already in their hands.

So what's in yours?

Maybe you've been the behind-the-scenes MVP for everyone else's dreams. Maybe you've been too exhausted to imagine anything new. Maybe life threw a curveball and you're still catching your breath. You don't need to wait until you have five extra hours a day or a six-month cushion in savings. Start where you are.

That might look like:

- Watching a free webinar on building a service-based business.

- Updating your LinkedIn headline so it reflects who you *are*, not just where you've been.

- Spending 30 minutes journaling the fears that whisper "not yet," then writing out three bold "what ifs" anyway.

- Asking a trusted friend to help you brainstorm five things people always come to you for.

Your side hustle doesn't have to start as a six-figure operation. It might start in your notes app, your voice memos, or your living room after dinner. Don't dismiss the seed just because it looks small. That seed might be your exit plan, your healing, or your legacy.

You don't have to know the whole path. Just commit to taking the first step.

The momentum comes later. The confidence catches up. The learning comes from doing. The magic multiplies. None of this happens until you begin.

## A Word for the Recovering Good Girls

If you're a Gen X woman of color, chances are you've spent a lifetime performing emotional labor in spaces that didn't always reciprocate your energy. You've been the reliable one. The fixer. The strong friend. The early-morning chauffeur, the late-night editor, the last-minute babysitter, the one who brings the extra charger, the snacks, and the calm voice of reason, even when you're unraveling on the inside.

You learned how to be useful. You mastered it. But here's the truth nobody told us in those "just be grateful" years: Being useful is not the same as being joyful. This next chapter is not about proving your worth. You've already done that, ten times over. This is about reclaiming your light, your softness, your wild ideas, and your yeses that are finally for *you*.

You do not need to earn rest. You do not need to explain joy. You do not need to apologize for needing more than survival.

The good girl in you was trained to say yes when you meant no, to smile when you wanted to scream, to dim your brilliance to make others comfortable. She got you here. Let's thank her... and retire her.

Janelle said it best: "Once I broke out of the box, I will not get boxed back in." That's the kind of energy this next season demands.

No more:

- Shrinking in rooms you were born to lead in.
- Waiting for permission to take up space.
- Pretending you're not wildly talented.

This is your official permission slip to stop betraying yourself in the name of being likable, safe, or easy to manage. That performance was tiring. And frankly, you're too grown for that.

This new chapter? It's about being bold, being brave, and being selfish, but in the best way. We're talking about the kind of selfishness that says, "I matter too." We want the kind of selfishness that reclaims time, energy, joy, boundaries, and curiosity.

So start where you are. I mean it. Start in spite of your messy desk and your uncertain heart. Start with your limited time. Start anyway.

Write the business plan, even if it's scribbled on the back of an old grocery list. Update your wardrobe, even if it's just adding lipstick and confidence. Rest on a Tuesday. Laugh until your stomach hurts. Say no without a paragraph of excuses.

I want you to expand. This is your time to reclaim and begin. This isn't about burning your life down. This is about choosing to rise, deliberately, audaciously, and beautifully.

Let this be the moment you draw the line and declare: I am no longer living life on default. I am designing it. Your next chapter is waiting. You're the only one who can write it.

# FINAL WORD

Go Be Her: If you've made it this far, it is time to pause.

Take a breath and let the weight of that accomplishment settle into your bones. You've done something sacred here. You didn't just skim through a book. You showed up for yourself. You turned the mirror inward. You reflected, wrestled, released, and remembered. You chose to believe, maybe for the first time in a long time, that more is still possible.

And now? You stand on the threshold of your next becoming. I know this place well. I've stood here myself, more than once.

I stood here when I left a job that no longer fit, even though the world told me it should be enough. I stood here when I traded in a big, beautiful house in the suburbs for a smaller space that felt more like me. I stood here when I launched a podcast and a business in my 50s, guided not by a detailed map, but by a deep knowing that my voice had value and my story had weight.

I didn't have all the answers. I still don't. But I had a vision. From that vision, I gave myself permission to follow it.

So now I pass the torch to you. You didn't think you spent all this time reading through these pages just for a feel-good fix, did you? No, my dear. This was your priming, all meant to spark your next phase. There is no more time for you to overthink it one second longer. You're ready, and this time won't last forever. When the day comes for you to leave this earth and dance into the hereafter, what hopes and dreams will die with you if you don't take this moment to bring them into existence? Yeah, I went there, and on purpose.

The whole point is that you don't need permission anymore. This midlife season is all about what you choose to do with it. You don't need to wait for the perfect plan or for everything to make sense. You just need to begin. Begin with what you know. Begin with what you feel. Begin with what lights you up.

Use the tools from these pages. Revisit the journal prompts when you feel stuck. Reread the stories when you need reminding of your strength. This book was never meant to be a one-time experience. It was always meant to be a companion, a homecoming, and a nudge back to yourself.

You are not starting over. You are starting from wisdom. That wisdom is shaped from grit, from joy, and from divine alignment. There's a whole world out there waiting for you to show up as your fullest self. Not the version shaped by guilt or duty or fear, but the version shaped by truth, courage, and desire.

Show them who you are now, not who you were taught to be. You can be who you choose to be. Do it on your terms and in your own style. Walk out into your new life with your head held high and your heart wide open.

Thank you for walking this path with me. I've poured myself into these pages, not just to teach, but to remind you of this. You are already enough. You are already worthy. Understand this more than anything else. You are more powerful than you've ever been taught to believe.

I see you.

Now, go be her.

With all my love and fire,

**Akilah**

***Your Next Chapter Begins Here***

## A Letter to Yourself

You've come a long way. You've reflected. You've released. You've remembered who you are.

Now it's time to declare what's next.

Use this space to write a letter to the *you* who is rising. The *you* who is done waiting. The *you* who is designing a life on purpose, with no apologies. Speak to her with love, clarity, and power. What does she need to hear from you right now? What promises are you ready to make to her? What future are you stepping into?

There are no rules. Just truth and love.

**Date:** _____

**Dear Me,**

*I'm so proud of how far you've come...*

*You've survived things that should have broken you. But they didn't.*

*You are allowed to want more now.*

*Here's what you are no longer carrying with you: _____.*

*Here's what you are walking toward: _____.*

*Here's who you are becoming: _____.*

*You don't have to do it all at once. But you do have to honor what you know is true.*

*So let this be your beginning. On your own terms.*

*You've got this.*

With love and fire,

_____

*(Your Signature)*

# SUPPORTING ARTICLES

American Institute for Economic Research. (2023). It's never too late: Changing careers at midlife. Psychology Today. https://www.psychologytoday.com/us/blog/from-both-sides-of-the-couch/202307/its-never-too-late-changing-careers-at-midlife

Baumeister, R. F., & Leary, M. R. (2023). Friendship quality and adult well-being: A systematic review across the PERMA model. Frontiers in Psychology, 14, Article 1059057. https://doi.org/10.3389/fpsyg.2023.1059057

Chopik, W. J., & Oh, J. (2024). The role of close friendships in self-rated health among older adults. International Journal of Psychology, 59(1), 41–53. https://doi.org/10.1002/ijop.13026

Clark, R., Davis, H., & Mitchell, O. S. (2021). Financial well-being among Black and Hispanic women [Report]. TIAA Institute. https://www.tiaa.org/public/institute/publication/2021/financial-well-being-among-black-and-hispanic-women

Cudjoe, T. K. M., Roth, D. L., Szanton, S. L., Wolff, J. L., Boyd, C. M., & Thorpe, R. J. (2020). The epidemiology of social isolation: National Health and Aging Trends Study. The Journals of Gerontology: Series B, 75(1), 107–113. https://doi.org/10.1093/geronb/gby037

Fingerman, K. L., Huo, M., & Kim, K. (2023). Intergenerational friendships and their role in reducing loneliness in later life. Verywell Health. Retrieved from https://www.verywellhealth.com/intergenerational-friendships-loneliness-6824319

Forbes. (2024, March 19). Changing jobs at midlife is good for your career—and your salary. Forbes. https://www.forbes.com/sites/avivahwittenbergcox/2024/03/19/changing-jobs-at-midlife-is-good-for-your-career--and-your-salary

Holt-Lunstad, J. (2020). The double pandemic of social isolation and COVID-19: Cross-sector policy must address both. Health Affairs Blog. https://doi.org/10.1377/forefront.20200609.53823

Labrague, L. J. (2023). Social support and psychological well-being during COVID-19 pandemic among Filipino adults: The mediating role of resilience. Frontiers in Psychology, 14, 1084992. https://doi.org/10.3389/fpsyg.2023.1084992

Lee, H. Y., & Stevens, D. (2023). Midlife financial strain and later-life health and wellbeing of husbands and wives: Linking and moderating roles of couple intimacy trajectories. PMC. https://www.ncbi.nlm.nih.gov/pmc/articles/PMC9851178/

Marcus, B. (2024, September 11). New report highlights how the financial burdens of Black women affect their mental health and career advancement. Forbes. https://www.forbes.com/sites/bonniemarcus/2024/09/11/new-report-highlights-how-the-financial-burdens-of-black-women-affect-their-mental-health-and-career-advancement/

Moya Vu, S., et al. (2023). Systematic review of racial/ethnic and gender differences in financial knowledge in the United States. Journal of Financial Literacy and Wellbeing. https://doi.org/10.1017/flw.2024.10

National Academies of Sciences, Engineering, and Medicine. (2020). Social isolation and loneliness in older adults: Opportunities for the health care system. The National Academies Press. https://doi.org/10.17226/25663

Pew Research Center. (2024, February 8). How Black Americans view financial success. https://www.pewresearch.org/2024/02/08/how-black-americans-view-financial-success/

Phoenix Insights & OECD. (2024). The rise of the second career among over-50s. The Times. https://www.thetimes.co.uk/article/thousands-of-over-50s-are-choosing-to-embark-on-a-second-career-in-an-entirely-new-field-s58wqhht3

Robinson, B. (2024, December 2). How to stay relevant in your career at midlife. Forbes. https://www.forbes.com/sites/bryanrobinson/2024/12/02/how-to-stay-relevant-in-your-career-at-midlife

Rolling Out. (2025, April 15). Career pivots lead to success for midlife professionals. Rolling Out. https://rollingout.com/2025/04/15/career-pivots-success-for-professionals

Sinek, S. (2025, January 24). Is this the 'ultimate biohack'? New York Post. https://nypost.com/2025/01/24/health/ultimate-biohack-could-help-you-live-longer-and-fight-stress/

Stokes, J. E., & Moorman, S. M. (2024). Friendship quality and depressive symptoms among midlife adults: Longitudinal evidence from MIDUS. PLOS ONE, 19(3), Article e0287452. https://doi.org/10.1371/journal.pone.0287452

van Tilburg, T. G., & Broese van Groenou, M. I. (2022). Changes in adult friendship networks between the 1970s and 2010s: Evidence from the Netherlands. Journal of Aging and Health, 34(10), 1476–1496. https://doi.org/10.1177/08982643221092991

Waldinger, R. J., & Schulz, M. S. (2023). The Good Life: Lessons from the world's longest scientific study of happiness. Simon & Schuster.

Wong, B. (2025, July 10). 'An uphill battle': Why are midlife men struggling to make – and keep – friends? The Guardian. https://www.theguardian.com/wellness/ng-interactive/2025/jul/10/male-friendships-midlife

# ABOUT THE AUTHOR

Dr. Akilah Willery is a digital education expert, midlife reinvention coach, and unapologetic truth-teller guiding a generation through their boldest pivots yet. With over two decades of leadership in instructional technology, professional learning, and digital transformation, Dr. Willery has become a trusted advisor to school districts, corporate teams, and career changers across the country.

But her story didn't stop with professional accolades and executive roles. At midlife, Akilah chose reinvention.

After years of helping others design powerful learning experiences, she turned the spotlight inward by downsizing her home, redesigning her life, and launching *Melanated Midlife*, a platform and podcast that empowers midlifers of color over 40 and 50 to reclaim their time, talents, and truth. Her signature blend of storytelling, strategy, and soulful honesty has resonated with an audience of high-achieving, heart-centered professionals who are ready to make moves, not excuses.

Akilah is not just a coach. She's a companion in the journey. Whether she's sharing personal stories of career pivots, the emotional process of decluttering a home filled with memories, or breaking down the myths of what "success" should look like after 50, her message is clear: *you're not too old, and it's not too late*.

Through her writing, workshops, courses, and coaching, Akilah helps midlife professionals embrace their right to change. She believes in starting where you are, using what you have, and building a life that finally feels like your own.

When she's not teaching, speaking, or coaching, you'll find her sipping a perfectly crafted latte, strolling through her favorite bookstore, or chilling in her beloved downsized home with her husband Brian. They have two sons, Brian II and Nicholas.

Dr. Willery holds a doctorate in educational leadership, plus certifications in technology and instructional design. But her greatest credentials? Reinventing herself and helping others do the same.

www.ingramcontent.com/pod-product-compliance
Lightning Source LLC
Chambersburg PA
CBHW060525150626
46550CB00019B/364